1st Workshop on Asian Translation (WAT 2014)

Tokyo, Japan
4 October 2014

ISBN: 978-1-5108-1399-1

Printed from e-media with permission by:

Curran Associates, Inc.
57 Morehouse Lane
Red Hook, NY 12571

Some format issues inherent in the e-media version may also appear in this print version.

Printed by Curran Associates, Inc. (2015)

For permission requests, please contact the Association for Computational Linguistics
at the address below.

Association for Computational Linguistics
209 N. Eighth Street
Stroudsburg, Pennsylvania 18360

Phone: 1-570-476-8006
Fax: 1-570-476-0860

acl@aclweb.org

Additional copies of this publication are available from:

Curran Associates, Inc.
57 Morehouse Lane
Red Hook, NY 12571 USA
Phone: 845-758-0400
Fax: 845-758-2634
Email: curran@proceedings.com
Web: www.proceedings.com

Proceedings of the 1st Workshop on Asian Translation (WAT2014)

Overview of the 1st Workshop on Asian Translation

Toshiaki Nakazawa
Japan Science and Technology Agency
nakazawa@pa.jst.jp

Hideya Mino
National Institute of Information and Communications Technology
hideya.mino@nict.go.jp

Isao Goto
NHK
goto.i-es@nhk.or.jp

Sadao Kurohashi
Kyoto University
kuro@i.kyoto-u.ac.jp

Eiichiro Sumita
National Institute of Information and Communications Technology
eiichiro.sumita@nict.go.jp

Abstract

This paper presents the results of the 1st workshop on Asian translation (WMT2014) shared tasks, which included J↔E translation subtasks and J↔C translation subtasks. As the first year of WAT, 12 institutions participated to the shared tasks. More than 300 translation results have been submitted to the automatic evaluation server, and selected submissions were manually evaluated.

1 Introduction

The Workshop on Asian Translation (WAT) is a new open evaluation campaign focusing on Asian languages. We would like to invite a broad range of participants and conduct various forms of machine translation experiments and evaluation. Collecting and sharing our knowledge will allow us to understand the essence of machine translation and the problems to be solved. We are working toward the practical use of machine translation among all Asian countries.

For the 1st WAT, we chose scientific papers as the targeted domain, and selected the languages Japanese, Chinese and English.

What makes WAT unique:

- Open innovation platform
  The test data is fixed and open, so you can repeat evaluations on the same data and confirm changes in translation accuracy over time. WAT has no deadline for the automatic translation quality evaluation (continuous evaluation), so you can submit translation results at any time.

- Domain and language pairs
  WAT is the world's first workshop that uses scientific papers as a domain and Japanese-Chinese as a language pair. In the future, we will add more Asian languages, such as Korean, Vietnamese, Indonesian, Thai, Myanmar and so on.

- Evaluation method
  Evaluation will be done by both automatic and human evaluation. For human evaluation, WAT will use crowdsourcing, which is low cost and allows multiple evaluations.

LangPair	Train	Dev	DevTest	Test
ASPEC-JE	3,008,500	1,790	1,784	1,812
ASPEC-JC	672,315	2,090	2,148	2,107

Table 1: Statistics of ASPEC.

2 Dataset

WAT uses Asian Scientific Paper Excerpt Corpus (ASPEC)[1] as the dataset. ASPEC is constructed by the Japan Science and Technology Agency (JST) in collaboration with the National Institute of Information and Communications Technology (NICT). It consists of a Japanese-English scientific paper abstract corpus (ASPEC-JE), which is used for J↔E subtasks, and a Japanese-Chinese scientific paper excerpt corpus (ASPEC-JC), which is used for J↔C subtasks. The statistics of each corpus are described in Table1.

2.1 ASPEC-JE

The training data of ASPEC-JE was constructed by the NICT from approximately 2 million Japanese-English scientific paper abstracts owned by the JST. Because the paper abstracts are kind

[1] http://lotus.kuee.kyoto-u.ac.jp/ASPEC/

Proceedings of the 1st Workshop on Asian Translation (WAT2014), pages 1–19,
Tokyo, Japan, 4th October 2014.

of comparable corpora, the sentence correspondences are automatically found using the method of (Utiyama and Isahara, 2007). Each sentence pair is accompanied with the similarity score and the field symbol. The similarity scores are calculated by the method of (Utiyama and Isahara, 2007). The field symbols are single letters A-Z and show the scientific field of each document[2]. The correspondance between the symbols and field names, along with the frequency and occurance ratios for the training data, are given in the README of ASPEC-JE.

The development, development-test and test data were extracted from parallel sentences from Japanese-English paper abstracts owned by JST that are not contained in the training data. Each data set contains 400 documents. Furthermore, the data has been selected to contain the same relative field coverage across each data set. The document alignment was conducted automatically and only documents with a 1-to-1 alignment are included. It is therefore possible to restore the original documents. The format is the same as for the training data except that there is no similarity score.

2.2 ASPEC-JC

ASPEC-JC is a parallel corpus consisting of Japanese scientific papers from the literature database and electronic journal site J-STAGE of JST that have been translated to Chinese after receiving permission from the necessary academic associations. The parts selected were abstracts and paragraph units from the body text, as these contain the highest overall vocabulary coverage.

The development, development-test and test data are extracted at random from documents containing single paragraphs across the entire corpus. Each set contains 400 paragraphs (documents). Therefore there are no documents sharing the same data across the training, development, development-test and test sets.

3 Baseline Systems

Human evaluations were conducted as pairwise comparisons between the translation results for a specific baseline system and translation results for each participant's system. That is, the specific baseline system was the standard of human evaluation. A phrase-based statistical machine translation (SMT) system was adopted as the specific baseline system at WAT 2014.

In addition to the results for the baseline phrase-based SMT system, we produced results for the baseline systems that consisted of a hierarchical phrase-based SMT system, a string-to-tree syntax-based SMT system, a tree-to-string syntax-based SMT system, five commercial rule-based machine translation (RBMT) systems, and two online translation systems. The SMT baseline systems consisted of publicly available software, and the procedures for building the systems and translating using the systems were published on the WAT 2014 web page[3]. We used Moses (Koehn et al., 2007; Hoang et al., 2009) as the implementation of the baseline SMT systems. The Berkeley parser (Petrov et al., 2006) was used to obtain syntactic annotations. The baseline systems are shown in Table 2.

The commercial RBMT systems and the online translation systems were operated by the organizers. We note that these RBMT companies and online translation companies did not submit themselves. Since our objective is not to compare commercial RBMT systems or online translation systems from companies that did not themselves participate, the system description of these systems are anonymized in this paper.

We describe the detail of the baseline SMT systems.

3.1 Data for Training

We used the following data for the training of the SMT baseline systems.

- Training data for the language model: All of the target language sentences in the parallel corpus.
- Training data for the translation model: Sentences that were 40 words or less in length. (For Japanese–English training data, we only used train-1.txt, which consisted of 1 million parallel sentence pairs with high similarity scores.)
- Development data for tuning: All of the development data.

3.2 Common Settings for Baseline SMT

We used the following tools for tokenization.

- Juman version 7.0[4] for Japanese segmentation.

[2] http://opac.jst.go.jp/bunrui/index.html

[3] http://lotus.kuee.kyoto-u.ac.jp/WAT/

[4] http://nlp.ist.i.kyoto-u.ac.jp/EN/index.php?JUMAN

System ID	System	Type	JE	EJ	JC	CJ
SMT Phrase	Moses' Phrase-based SMT	SMT	✓	✓	✓	✓
SMT Hiero	Moses' Hierarchical Phrase-based SMT	SMT	✓	✓	✓	✓
SMT S2T	Moses' String-to-Tree Syntax-based SMT and Berkeley parser	SMT	✓		✓	
SMT T2S	Moses' Tree-to-String Syntax-based SMT and Berkeley parser	SMT		✓		✓
RBMT X	The Honyaku V15 (Commercial system)	RBMT	✓	✓		
RBMT X	ATLAS V14 (Commercial system)	RBMT	✓	✓		
RBMT X	PAT-Transer 2009 (Commercial system)	RBMT	✓	✓		
RBMT X	J-Beijing 7 (Commercial system)	RBMT			✓	✓
RBMT X	Hohrai 2011 (Commercial system)	RBMT			✓	✓
Online X	Google translate (July, 2014)	(SMT)	✓	✓	✓	✓
Online X	Bing translator (July, 2014)	(SMT)	✓	✓	✓	✓

Table 2: Baseline Systems

- Stanford Word Segmenter version 2014-01-04[5] (Chinese Penn Treebank (CTB) model) for Chinese segmentation.
- The Moses toolkit for English tokenization.

To obtain word alignments, GIZA++ and grow-diag-final-and heuristics were used. We used 5-gram language models with modified Kneser-Ney smoothing, which were built using a tool in the Moses toolkit (Heafield et al., 2013).

3.3 Phrase-based SMT

We used the following Moses' configuration for the phrase-based SMT system.

- distortion-limit = 20
- msd-bidirectional-fe lexicalized reordering
- Phrase score option: GoodTuring

The default values were used for the other system parameters.

3.4 Hierarchical Phrase-based SMT

We used the following Moses' configuration for the hierarchical phrase-based SMT system.

- max-chart-span = 1000
- Phrase score option: GoodTuring

The default values were used for the other system parameters.

3.5 String-to-Tree Syntax-based SMT

We used Berkeley parser to obtain target language syntax. We used the following Moses' configuration for the string-to-tree syntax-based SMT system.

- max-chart-span = 1000
- Phrase score option: GoodTuring
- Phrase extraction options: MaxSpan = 1000, MinHoleSource = 1, and NonTermConsecSource.

The default values were used for the other system parameters.

3.6 Tree-to-String Syntax-based SMT

We used Berkeley parser to obtain source language syntax. We used the following Moses' configuration for the baseline tree-to-string syntax-based SMT system.

- max-chart-span = 1000
- Phrase score option: GoodTuring
- Phrase extraction options: MaxSpan = 1000, MinHoleSource = 1, MinWords = 0, NonTermConsecSource, and AllowOnlyUnalignedWords.

The default values were used for the other system parameters.

4 Automatic Evaluation

4.1 Procedure of Calculating Automatic Evaluation Score

We calculated automatic evaluation scores of the translation results applying two popular metrics: BLEU (Papineni et al., 2002) and RIBES (Isozaki et al., 2010). BLEU scores were calculated with *multi-bleu.perl* distributed with the Moses toolkit (Koehn et al., 2007). RIBES scores were calculated with *RIBES.py* version 1.02.4 [6]. All scores of each task were calculated using one reference. Before the calculation of the automatic evaluation scores, the translation results have been tokenized with word segmentation tools on each language.

[5] http://nlp.stanford.edu/software/segmenter.shtml

[6] http://www.kecl.ntt.co.jp/icl/lirg/ribes/index.html

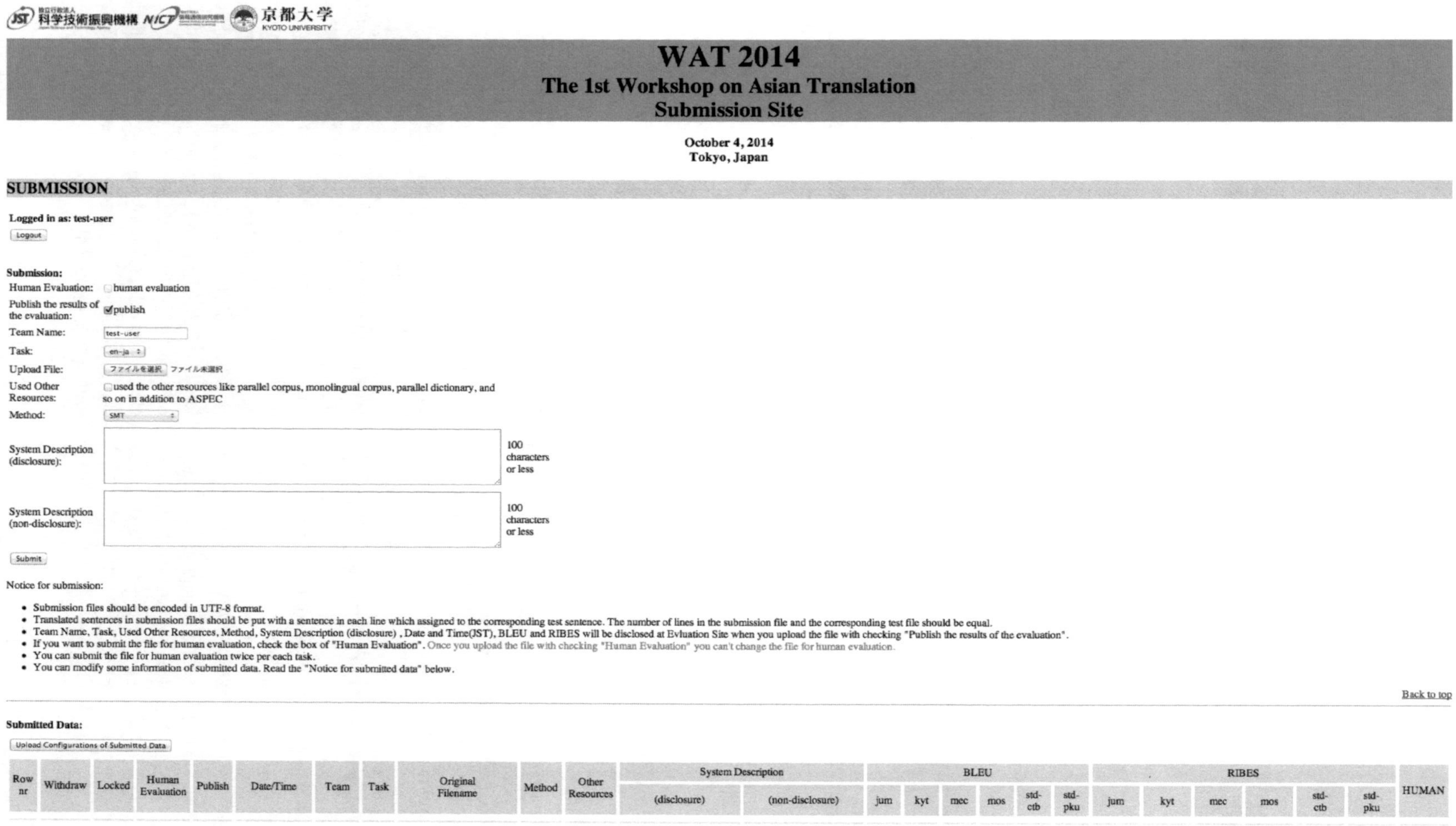

Figure 1: The submission web page for participants

For Japanese segmentation we use three different tools, which are Juman version 7.0 (Kurohashi et al., 1994), KyTea 0.4.6 (Neubig et al., 2011) with Full SVM model [7] and MeCab 0.996 (Kudo, 2005) with IPA dictionary 2.7.0 [8]. For Chinese segmentation we use two different tools, which are KyTea 0.4.6 with Full SVM Model in MSR model and Stanford Word Segmenter version 2014-06-16 with Chinese Penn Treebank (CTB) and Peking University (PKU) model [9] (Tseng, 2005). For English segmentation we use tokenizer.perl [10] in the Moses toolkit.

The detailed procedures for the automatic evaluation are shown at WAT2014 evaluation web page [11].

4.2 Automatic Evaluation System

The participants submit the translation results via an automatic evaluation system deployed at WAT2014 web page, which give them automatic evaluation scores of the results they upload. Figure 1 shows the submitting interface for participants. The system requires the participants to provide the following information when they upload the translation results:

- Subtask ($J \leftrightarrow E$, $J \leftrightarrow C$)
- Method (SMT, RBMT, SMT and RBMT, EBMT, Other)
- Existence of the use of other resources in addition to ASPEC
- Permission of publishing the automatic evaluation scores on WAT2014 web page

The server of the system keeps all submitted information including translation results or scores and participants can confirm the only information they uploaded. The information of translation results which the participant permits to publish is disclosed on the web page. In addition to submitting the translation results for automatic evaluation, participants submit the results for human evaluation with the same web interface. This automatic evaluation system will be available even after WAT2014. Everybody can use the system by registering on the registration web page [12].

5 Human Evaluation

5.1 Using Crowdsourcing

As all the MT researchers know, the human evaluation costs a lot of time and money. One of the solutions to reduce them is using crowdsourcing. Other machine translation evaluation campaigns such as IWSLT (2011, 2012) and WMT (2012, 2013) also used crowdsourcing for the human evaluation. Recently, there are so many crowdsourcing services in the world: Amazon Mechanical Turk[13], CrowdFlower[14], Yahoo Crowdsourcing[15], Lancers[16] and so on. Among these services, we used Lancers for the human evaluation of WAT2014.

There are two reasons of choosing Lancers. One is that we can set the category of the crowdsourcing task ('Translation' for this case). We can reach the appropriate workers by setting the appropriate categories. The other reason is that we can ask the task to the identity-verified workers. This function guarantee the quality of the workers. These two advantages can keep the evaluation quality at higher level.

5.2 Human Evaluation Method

For the human evaluation, we randomly chose *documents* from the Test set of ASPEC data, in total 400 sentence pairs for JE and JC. We excluded the documents which contains a sentence with longer than 100 Japanese characters. Each submission is compared with the baseline translation (Phrase-based SMT, described in Section 3) and given *HUMAN* score.

5.2.1 Pairwise Evaluation of Sentences

We conducted pairwise evaluation of each test sentence of the 400 sentences. The input sentence and two translations (the baseline and a submission) are shown to the workers, and the workers are asked to judge which translation is better than the other, or they are of the same quality. The order of the two translations are at random. Figure 2 shows the illustration of the evaluation.

[7] http://www.phontron.com/kytea/model.html
[8] http://code.google.com/p/mecab/downloads/detail?name=mecab-ipadic-2.7.0-20070801.tar.gz
[9] http://nlp.stanford.edu/software/segmenter.shtml
[10] https://github.com/moses-smt/mosesdecoder/tree/RELEASE-2.1.1/scripts/tokenizer/tokenizer.perl
[11] http://lotus.kuee.kyoto-u.ac.jp/WAT/evaluation/index.html
[12] http://lotus.kuee.kyoto-u.ac.jp/WAT/registration/index.html
[13] https://www.mturk.com
[14] http://www.crowdflower.com
[15] http://crowdsourcing.yahoo.co.jp (Japanese service)
[16] http://www.lancers.jp (Japanese service)

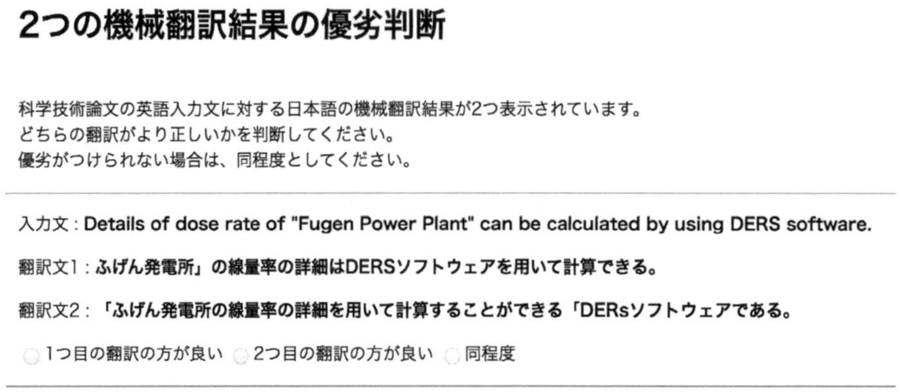

Figure 2: The illustration of the crowdsourcing evaluation. The workers are asked to judge which translation is better, or the same.

Worker 1	A	A	A	A	A	A	Tie	Tie	Tie	B
Worker 2	A	A	A	Tie	Tie	B	Tie	Tie	B	B
Worker 3	A	Tie	B	Tie	B	B	Tie	B	B	B
Decision	A	A	A	A	Tie	B	Tie	B	B	B

Table 3: The combinations of human judgements and the final decision of each sentence pairs from system A and B.

5.2.2 Voting

The crowdsourcing workers are not specialists, thus the quality of the judgements are not necessarily precise. To guarantee the quality of the evaluation, each sentence is evaluated by 3 different workers and the final decision is made by the voting of the judgements. Table 3 shows all the combinations of the worker judgements and the final decision.

5.2.3 HUMAN Score Calculation

Suppose W to be the number of *wins* compared to the baseline, L to be the number of *losses* and T to be the number of *ties*, the HUMAN score, which is the official human evaluation score of WAT2014, can be calculated by the following formula:

$$HUMAN = 100 \times \frac{W - L}{W + L + T}$$

From the definition, the HUMAN score ranges between -100 and 100.

5.2.4 Confidence Interval Estimation

As there are several ways to estimate the confidence interval, we chose the bootstrap resampling (Koehn, 2004) to estimated 95% confidence interval. The procedure is as follows:

1. randomly select 300 sentences from the 400 human evaluation sentences, and calculate the HUMAN score on the selected sentences
2. iterate the previous step 1000 times and get 1000 HUMAN scores
3. sort the 1000 scores and estimate the 95% confidence interval by discarding top and bottom 25 scores

5.3 Cost of Evaluation

One big benefit of using crowdsourcing is that we can reduce the cost of evaluations. In WAT2014, one judgement costs 5 JPY. The evaluation of a submission requires 3 (judgements) × 400 (sentence pairs) = 1,200 judgements and it costs 5 × 1,200 = 6,000 JPY. The time for the evaluation differs depending on the translation direction. On the average, one evaluation finished in a couple of days.

6 Participants List

Table 4 shows the list of participants to WAT2014. There are not only the Japanese organizations, but some organizations came from outside Japan. 12 teams submitted one or more translation results to the automatic evaluation server, and 11 teams submitted one or more translation results to the human evaluation.

7 Evaluation Results

In this section, the evaluation results of WAT2014 are reported from several perspectives. Parts of the results of both automatic and human evaluations are also accessible at WAT2014 website[17].

7.1 Official Automatic Evaluation Results

Figure 3 shows the official automatic evaluation results of the representative submissions and baseline systems. The automatic evaluation results of all the submissions are shown in Section Appendix A.

7.2 Official Human Evaluation Results

HUMAN scores

Figure 4 shows the official human evaluation results. The error bars in the figures show the 95% confidence interval (see Section 5.2.4). Note that overlapping the error bars between two submissions does not necessarily mean that there is no significant difference. If an error bar crosses the x-axis (HUMAN score = 0), it means that there is no significant difference between the submission and the baseline (SMT Phrase).

From the results, the followings can be observed:

- The best SMT system achieved better quality than RBMT system.
- The translation quality of the widely used systems was Phrase-based SMT < Hierarchical PBSMT < Syntax-based SMT (S2T and T2S).
- Forest-to-String Syntax-based SMT system (Neubig, 2014) achieved the best quality for all the translation directions.

Statistical Significance Testing between Submissions

Tables 5, 6, 7 and 8 show the results of statistical significance testings of JE, EJ, JC and CJ translations respectively where all the pairs of submissions are tested. $\ggg$, $\gg$ and $>$ mean that the system in the row is *better* than the system in the column by $p < 0.01, 0.05, 0.1$ respectively. The testings are also done by the bootstrap resampling as follows:

1. randomly select 300 sentences from the 400 human evaluation sentences, and calculate the HUMAN scores on the selected sentences for both systems
2. iterate the previous step 1000 times and count the number of wins (W), losses (L) and ties (T)
3. calculate $p = \frac{L}{W+L}$

Inter-annotator Agreement

To assess the reliability of agreement between the crowdsourcing workers, we calculated the Fleiss' kappa (Fleiss and others, 1971) values. The results are shown in Table 9. We can see that the Kappa values are larger for X $\rightarrow$ J translations than J $\rightarrow$ X translations. This may be because we used Japanese crowdsourcing service for the evaluation and the majority of the crowdsourcing workers are Japanese. The MT evaluation of their mother tongue is much easier than the others in general.

Case Study: Direct Comparison and Relative Comparison

Looking at evaluation results of WEBLIO-EJ1 1 and 2 submissions (see Table 12), the automatic and human evaluations are inconsistent: the WEBLIO-EJ1 2 is consistently better than WEBLIO-EJ1 1 in the automatic evaluation, however it is much worse in the human evaluation. According to the descriptions of the two submissions, the difference of the two is whether it uses the forest input or not. It is natural that using the forest input improves the translation quality, thus we conducted the human evaluation of WEBLIO-EJ1 2 compared to WEBLIO-EJ1 1, which means we used WEBLIO-EJ1 1 as the baseline for the human evaluation.

The HUMAN score was 2.50 $\pm$ 4.17 which means there is no significant difference between the two, and this result is far from the results of the official results. Actually, taking the confidence intervals into consideration, this conclusion can be derived under some probability.

The Fleiss' kappa value was 0.528 and it is much higher than the other E$\rightarrow$J human evaluations. This may be because the outputs of the two systems are quite similar and it is very easy for the

[17] http://lotus.kuee.kyoto-u.ac.jp/WAT/evaluation/index.html

	non-removal	removal
JE BLEU	0.46489	0.95098
JE RIBES	0.78255	0.83691
EJ BLEU	0.41524	0.84418
EJ RIBES	0.75105	0.85730
JC BLEU	0.49240	0.07937
JC RIBES	0.38695	0.10198
CJ BLEU	0.78713	0.82592
CJ RIBES	0.70081	0.83209

Table 10: The changes of correlations (R^2) before and after removing RBMT and online systems.

workers to judge which translation is better. If two translations have both better and worse parts than the other, the workers would evaluate differently from person to person.

7.3 Correlation between Automatic and Human Evaluations

Figure 5 shows the correlations between automatic evaluation measures (BLEU/RIBES) and the HUMAN score. It is well known that the automatic and human evaluations do not have good correlations for RBMT and online systems. Removing these systems from the graph changes the correlation values (R^2) like in Table 10. The correlation becomes much better after removing the RBMT and online systems for all the translation directions other than J→C.

8 Submitted Data

The number of published automatic evaluaition results of 12 teams exceeded 100 by the day of WAT2014 workshop and 37 translation results for human evaluation was submitted by 11 teams. We will organize the all submitted data for human evaluation and make it public.

9 Conclusion and Future Perspective

This paper summarized the WAT2014 machine translation evaluation campaing. We had 12 participants worldwide, and collected a large number of submissions which are useful to improve the current machine translation systems by analyzing the submissions and finding the issues.

For the next WAT workshop, we are planning to conduct context-aware MT evaluations. The test data of WAT is prepared using the paragraph as a unit, while almost all other evaluation campaigns use the sentence as a unit. Therefore, it is suitable to investigate the importance of the context for the translation.

Also, we are very happy to include other languages if there are available resources.

Appendix A Submissions

Tables 11, 12, 13 and 14 summarize all the submissions listed in the automatic evaluation server at the point of WAT2014 workshop (4th, October, 2014). The OTHER RESOURCES column shows the use of other resources such as parallel corpora, monolingual corpora and parallel dictionaries in addition to ASPEC.

Team ID	Organization	JE	EJ	JC	CJ
NAIST (Neubig, 2014)	Nara Institute of Science and Technology	✓	✓	✓	✓
EIWA (Ehara, 2014)	Yamanashi Eiwa College	✓			✓
Kyoto-U (Richardson et al., 2014)	Kyoto University	✓	✓	✓	✓
WEBLIO-EJ1 (Zhu, 2014)	Weblio, Inc.		✓		
TMU (Ohwada et al., 2014)	Tokyo Metropolitan University	✓			
BJTUNLP (Cai et al., 2014)	Beijing Jiaotong University			✓	
NII (Hoshino et al., 2014)	National Institute of Informatics	✓			
SAS_MT (Wang et al., 2014)	SAS Research and Development Co., Ltd		✓		✓
Sense (Tan and Bond, 2014)	Saarland University & Nanyang Technological University	✓	✓	✓	✓
NICT (Ding et al., 2014)	National Institute of Information and Communication Technology			✓	
TOSHIBA (Sonoh et al., 2014)	Toshiba Corporation	✓		✓	
WASUIPS (Yang and Lepage, 2014)	Waseda University			✓*	✓*

Table 4: The list of participants which submitted translation results to WAT2014 and their participations to each subtasks. (*Only submitted to automatic evaluations.)

	NAIST 2	Kyoto-U 1	SMT S2T	TOSHIBA 1	RBMT D	EIWA	Kyoto-U 2	TOSHIBA 2	Online D	SMT Hiero	Sense	NII 1	NII 2	TMU 1	TMU 2
NAIST 1	-	⋙	⋙	⋙	⋙	⋙	⋙	⋙	⋙	⋙	⋙	⋙	⋙	⋙	⋙
NAIST 2		⋙	⋙	⋙	⋙	⋙	⋙	⋙	⋙	⋙	⋙	⋙	⋙	⋙	⋙
Kyoto-U 1			-	-	-	-	-	>	⋙	⋙	⋙	⋙	⋙	⋙	⋙
SMT S2T				-	-	-	>	>	⋙	⋙	⋙	⋙	⋙	⋙	⋙
TOSHIBA 1					-	-	-	-	⋙	⋙	⋙	⋙	⋙	⋙	⋙
RBMT D						-	-	-	⋙	⋙	⋙	⋙	⋙	⋙	⋙
EIWA							-	-	⋙	⋙	⋙	⋙	⋙	⋙	⋙
Kyoto-U 2								-	⋙	⋙	⋙	⋙	⋙	⋙	⋙
TOSHIBA 2									≫	⋙	⋙	⋙	⋙	⋙	⋙
Online D										≫	⋙	⋙	⋙	⋙	⋙
SMT Hiero											≫	⋙	⋙	⋙	⋙
Sense												≫	⋙	⋙	⋙
NII 1													⋙	⋙	⋙
NII 2														-	-
TMU 1															-

Table 5: Statistical significance testing of JE results.

	NAIST 2	WEBLIO-EJ1 1	Online A	Kyoto-U 1	WEBLIO-EJ1 2	SMT T2S	Kyoto-U 2	SMT Hiero	SAS_MT	Sense	RBMT B
NAIST 1	≫	⋙	⋙	⋙	⋙	⋙	⋙	⋙	⋙	⋙	⋙
NAIST 2		⋙	⋙	⋙	⋙	⋙	⋙	⋙	⋙	⋙	⋙
WEBLIO-EJ1 1			-	≫	⋙	⋙	⋙	⋙	⋙	⋙	⋙
Online A				>	≫	⋙	⋙	⋙	⋙	⋙	⋙
Kyoto-U 1					-	>	≫	≫	⋙	⋙	⋙
WEBLIO-EJ1 2						-	-	>	⋙	⋙	⋙
SMT T2S							-	-	≫	⋙	⋙
Kyoto-U 2								-	≫	⋙	⋙
SMT Hiero									>	⋙	⋙
SAS_MT										⋙	⋙
Sense											-

Table 6: Statistical significance testing of EJ results.

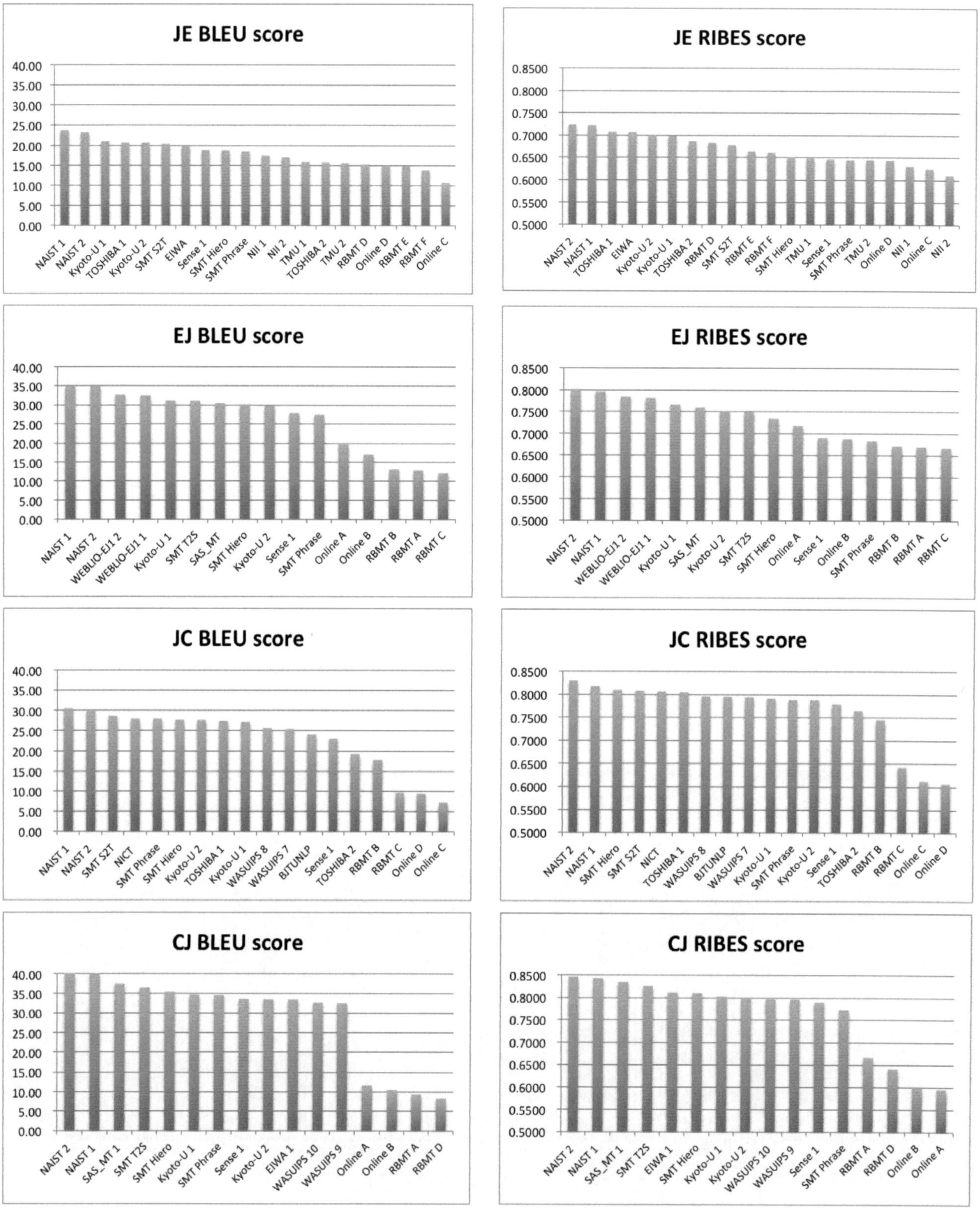

Figure 3: The official automatic evaluation results.

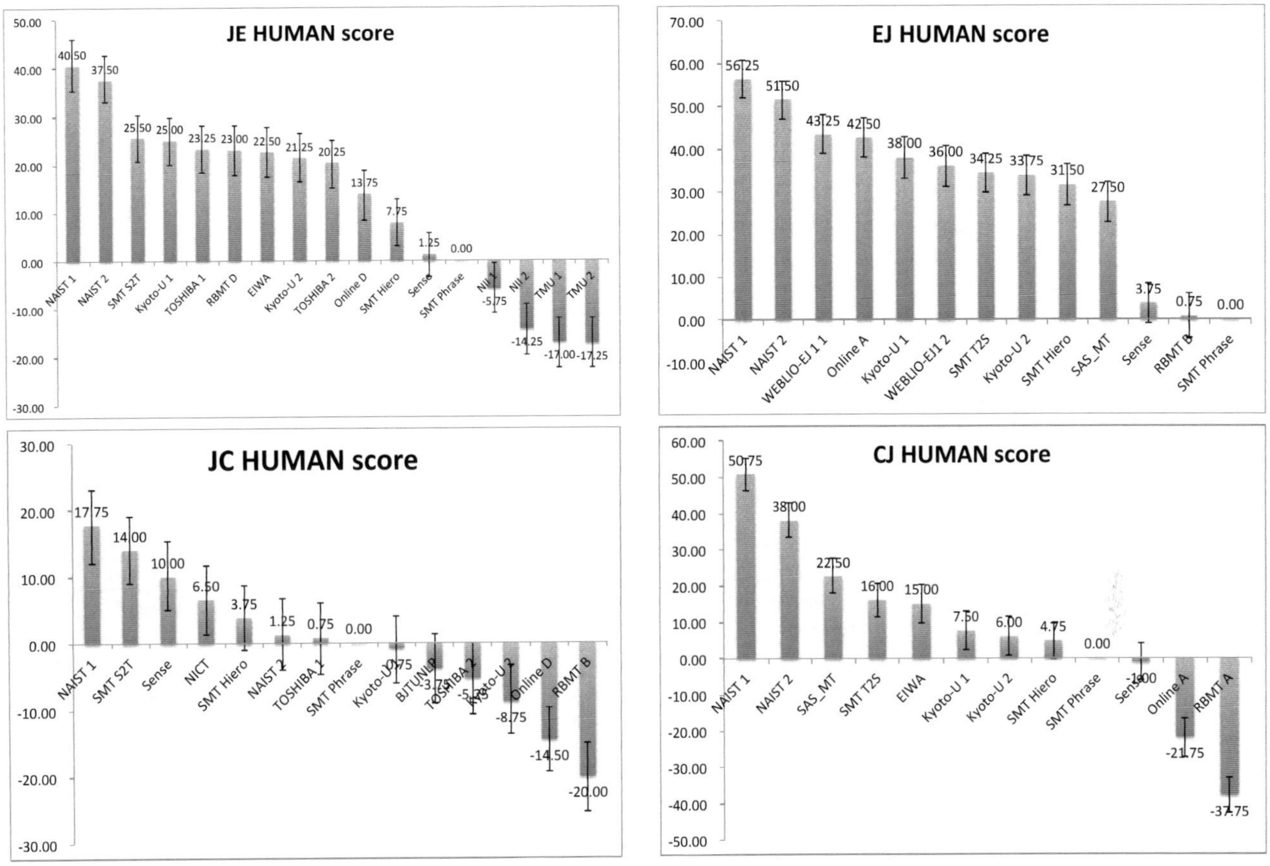

Figure 4: The official human evaluation results.

	SMT S2T	Sense	NICT	SMT Hiero	NAIST 2	TOSHIBA 1	Kyoto-U 1	BJTUNLP	TOSHIBA 2	Kyoto-U 2	Online D	RBMT B
NAIST 1	-	⋙	⋙	⋙	⋙	⋙	⋙	⋙	⋙	⋙	⋙	⋙
SMT S2T		-	≫	⋙	⋙	⋙	⋙	⋙	⋙	⋙	⋙	⋙
Sense			-	≫	⋙	⋙	⋙	⋙	⋙	⋙	⋙	⋙
NICT				-	>	≫	≫	⋙	⋙	⋙	⋙	⋙
SMT Hiero					-	-	-	≫	⋙	⋙	⋙	⋙
NAIST 2						-	-	>	≫	⋙	⋙	⋙
TOSHIBA 1							-	>	≫	⋙	⋙	⋙
Kyoto-U 1								-	>	⋙	⋙	⋙
BJTUNLP									-	>	⋙	⋙
TOSHIBA 2										-	⋙	⋙
Kyoto-U 2											≫	⋙
Online D												>

Table 7: Statistical significance testing of JC results.

	NAIST 2	SAS_MT	SMT T2S	EIWA	Kyoto-U 1	Kyoto-U 2	SMT Hiero	Sense	Online A	RBMT A
NAIST 1	⋙	⋙	⋙	⋙	⋙	⋙	⋙	⋙	⋙	⋙
NAIST 2		⋙	⋙	⋙	⋙	⋙	⋙	⋙	⋙	⋙
SAS_MT			≫	≫	⋙	⋙	⋙	⋙	⋙	⋙
SMT T2S				-	⋙	⋙	⋙	⋙	⋙	⋙
EIWA					⋙	⋙	⋙	⋙	⋙	⋙
Kyoto-U 1						-	-	⋙	⋙	⋙
Kyoto-U 2							-	≫	⋙	⋙
SMT Hiero								≫	⋙	⋙
Sense									⋙	⋙
Online A										⋙

Table 8: Statistical significance testing of CJ results.

JE

System ID	Kappa
NAIST 1	0.162
NAIST 2	0.047
SMT S2T	0.099
Kyoto-U 1	0.070
TOSHIBA 1	0.098
RBMT D	0.075
EIWA	0.083
Kyoto-U 2	0.139
TOSHIBA 2	0.078
Online D	0.055
SMT Hiero	0.119
Sense	0.245
NII 1	0.119
NII 2	0.086
TMU 1	0.091
TMU 2	0.136
ave.	0.106

EJ

System ID	Kappa
NAIST 1	0.280
NAIST 2	0.250
WEBLIO-EJ1 1	0.238
Online A	0.219
Kyoto-U 1	0.216
WEBLIO-EJ1 2	0.240
SMT T2S	0.240
Kyoto-U 2	0.229
SMT Hiero	0.277
SAS_MT	0.248
Sense	0.395
RBMT B	0.217
ave.	0.254

JC

System ID	Kappa
NAIST 1	0.077
SMT S2T	0.069
Sense	0.087
NICT	0.066
SMT Hiero	0.202
NAIST 2	0.093
TOSHIBA 1	0.089
Kyoto-U 1	0.091
BJTUNLP	0.198
TOSHIBA 2	0.066
Kyoto-U 2	0.163
Online D	0.035
RBMT B	0.083
ave.	0.101

CJ

System ID	Kappa
NAIST 1	0.168
NAIST 2	0.203
SAS_MT	0.167
SMT T2S	0.236
EIWA	0.175
Kyoto-U 1	0.199
Kyoto-U 2	0.180
SMT Hiero	0.274
Sense	0.228
Online A	0.239
RBMT A	0.130
ave.	0.200

Table 9: The Fleiss' kappa values of human evaluation results.

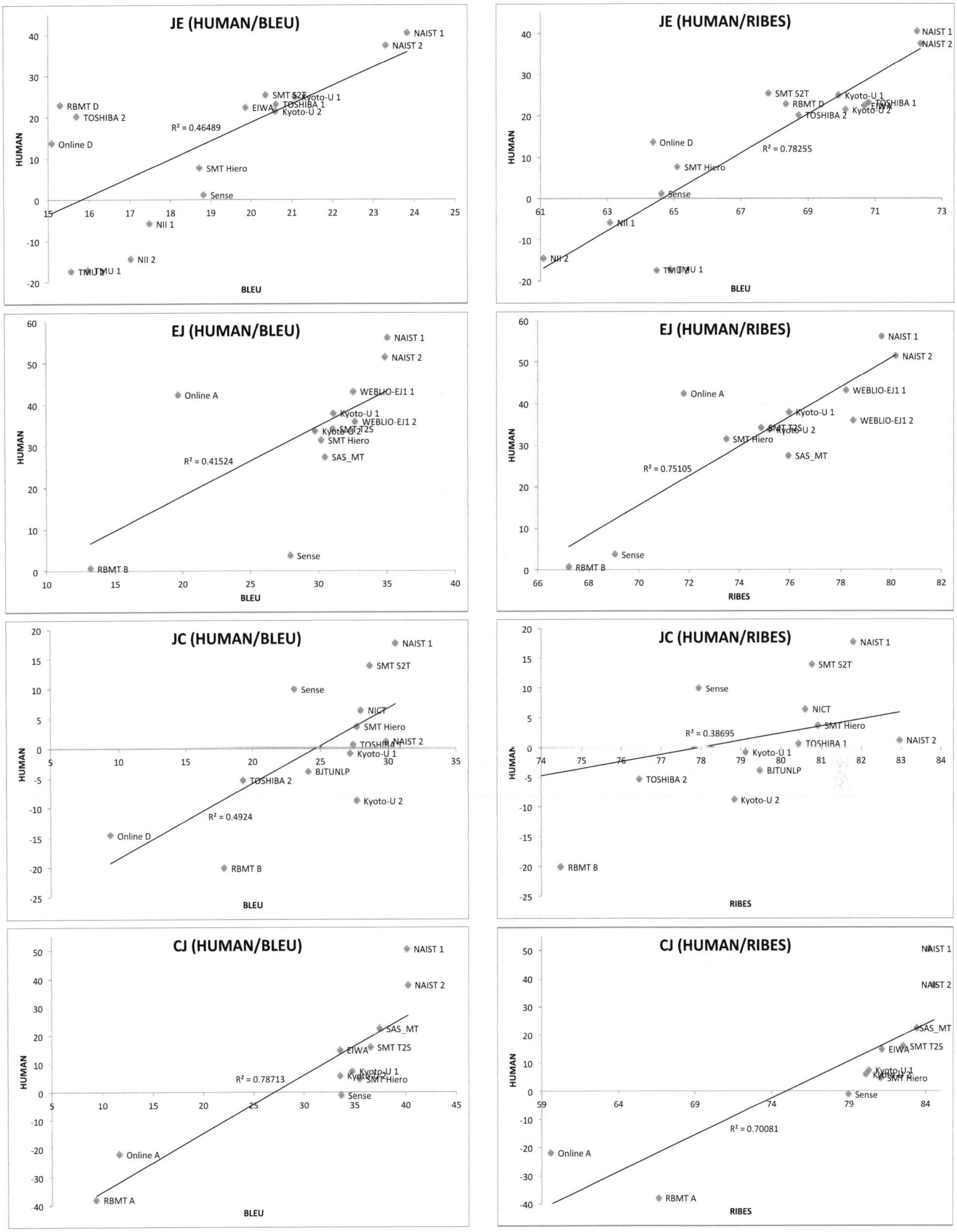

Figure 5: The correlations between BLEU/RIBES and HUMAN scores.

SYSTEM ID	ID	METHOD	OTHER RESOURCES	BLEU	RIBES	HUMAN	SYSTEM DESCRIPTION
SMT Hiero	2	SMT	NO	18.72	0.651066	+7.75	Hierarchical Phrase-based SMT
SMT Phrase	6	SMT	NO	18.45	0.645137	—	Phrase-based SMT
SMT S2T	9	SMT	NO	20.36	0.678253	+25.50	String-to-Tree SMT
Online D	35	Other	YES	15.08	0.643588	+13.75	Online D
RBMT E	76	Other	YES	14.82	0.663851	—	RBMT E
RBMT F	79	Other	YES	13.86	0.661387	—	RBMT F
Online C	87	Other	YES	10.64	0.624827	—	Online C
RBMT D	96	Other	YES	15.29	0.683378	+23.00	RBMT D
NAIST 1	46	SMT	YES	23.82	0.722599	+40.50	Travatar-based Forest-to-String SMT System with Extra Dictionaries
NAIST 2	119	SMT	NO	23.29	0.723541	+37.50	Travatar-based Forest-to-String SMT System
NAIST 3	125	SMT	NO	23.47	0.723670	—	Travatar-based Forest-to-String SMT System (Tuned BLEU+RIBES)
EIWA	116	SMT and RBMT	YES	19.86	0.706686	+22.50	Combination of RBMT and SPE(statistical post editing)
Kyoto-U 3	136	EBMT	NO	20.02	0.689829	—	Our baseline system using 3M parallel sentences
Kyoto-U 2	256	EBMT	NO	20.60	0.701154	+21.25	Our new baseline system after several modifications
Kyoto-U 1	262	EBMT	NO	21.07	0.698953	+25.00	Our new baseline system after several modifications + 20-best parses, KN7, RNNLM reranking
TMU 2	300	SMT	NO	15.55	0.644698	-17.25	Our baseline system with preordering method
TMU 1	301	SMT	NO	15.95	0.648879	-17.20	Our baseline system with another preordering method
TMU 3	307	SMT	NO	15.40	0.613119	—	Our baseline system
NII 1	271	SMT	NO	17.47	0.630825	-5.75	Our Baseline
NII 2	272	SMT	NO	17.01	0.610833	-14.25	Our Baseline with Preordering
Sense 1	164	SMT	NO	18.82	0.646204	+1.25	Paraphrase max10
Sense 2	185	SMT	NO	18.57	0.640393	—	Baseline SMT
Sense 3	191	SMT	NO	18.00	0.641377	—	Context sensitive SMT
Sense 4	205	SMT	NO	18.87	0.646133	—	SMT with lexicon
Sense 5	206	SMT	NO	18.91	0.637375	—	SMT with lexicon X5
TOSHIBA 2	240	RBMT	YES	15.69	0.687122	+20.25	RBMT system
TOSHIBA 1	241	SMT and RBMT	YES	20.61	0.707936	+23.25	RBMT with SPE(Statistical Post Editing) system

Table 11: JE submissions

SYSTEM ID	ID	METHOD	OTHER RESOURCES	BLEU			RIBES			HUMAN	SYSTEM DESCRIPTION
				juman	kytea	mecab	juman	kytea	mecab		
SMT Phrase	5	SMT	NO	27.48	29.80	28.27	0.683735	0.691926	0.695390	——	Phrase-based SMT
SMT T2S	12	SMT	NO	31.05	33.44	32.10	0.748883	0.758031	0.760516	+34.25	Tree-to-String SMT
Online A	34	Other	YES	19.66	21.63	20.17	0.718019	0.723486	0.725848	+42.50	Online A
RBMT B	66	Other	YES	13.18	14.85	13.48	0.671958	0.680748	0.682683	+0.75	RBMT B
RBMT A	68	Other	YES	12.86	14.43	13.16	0.670167	0.676464	0.678934	——	RBMT A
Online B	91	Other	YES	17.04	18.67	17.36	0.687797	0.693390	0.698126	——	Online B
RBMT C	95	Other	YES	12.19	13.32	12.14	0.668372	0.672645	0.676018	——	RBMT C
SMT Hiero	367	SMT	NO	30.19	32.56	30.94	0.734705	0.746978	0.747722	+31.50	Hierarchical Phrase-based SMT
NAIST 1	118	SMT	NO	35.03	37.16	35.81	0.796079	0.801520	0.806581	+56.25	Travatar-based Forest-to-String SMT System
NAIST 2	126	SMT	NO	34.84	37.15	35.67	0.801742	0.807010	0.811081	+51.50	Travatar-based Forest-to-String SMT System (Tuned BLEU+RIBES)
Kyoto-U 3	134	EBMT	NO	28.93	31.61	29.59	0.743969	0.755744	0.756545	——	Our baseline system using 3M parallel sentences
Kyoto-U 4	186	EBMT	NO	30.25	32.78	30.84	0.755629	0.765251	0.766495	——	Using n-best parses and RNNLM
Kyoto-U 2	253	EBMT	NO	29.76	32.46	30.46	0.752058	0.764049	0.766435	+33.75	Our new baseline system after several modifications
Kyoto-U 1	267	EBMT	NO	31.09	33.55	31.73	0.766435	0.770908	0.771545	+38.00	Our new baseline system after several modifications + 20-best parses, KN7, RNNLM reranking
WEBLIO-EJ1 1	132	SMT	NO	32.53	34.87	33.26	0.782066	0.786902	0.792616	+43.25	Weblio Pre-reordering SMT System Baseline
WEBLIO-EJ1 2	202	SMT	NO	32.69	35.04	33.40	0.785015	0.790066	0.795027	+36.00	Weblio Pre-reordering SMT System (with forest inputs)
SAS_MT	264	SMT	NO	30.47	33.00	31.47	0.759415	0.770948	0.771605	+27.50	Syntactic reordering Hierarchical SMT (using part of data)
Sense 2	163	SMT	NO	27.88	30.27	28.72	0.690718	0.699334	0.703139	——	Paraphrase max10
Sense 1	184	SMT	NO	27.92	30.18	28.66	0.690464	0.700583	0.703049	+3.75	Baseline SMT
Sense 3	190	SMT	NO	26.59	28.46	27.15	0.684467	0.694678	0.697257	——	Context sensitive SMT
Sense 4	265	SMT	NO	27.00	29.15	27.81	0.681194	0.689623	0.693560	——	SMT with 20x lexicon
Sense 5	274	SMT	NO	27.33	29.54	28.16	0.679666	0.688801	0.691011	——	SMT with lexicon X5

Table 12: EJ submissions

SYSTEM ID	ID	METHOD	OTHER RESOURCES	BLEU			RIBES			HUMAN	SYSTEM DESCRIPTION
				kytea	stanford (ctb)	stanford (pku)	kytea	stanford (ctb)	stanford (pku)		
SMT Hiero	3	SMT	NO	27.71	27.70	27.35	0.809128	0.809561	0.811394	+3.75	Hierarchical Phrase-based SMT
SMT Phrase	7	SMT	NO	27.96	28.01	27.68	0.788961	0.790263	0.790937	—	Phrase-based SMT
SMT S2T	10	SMT	NO	28.65	28.65	28.35	0.807606	0.809457	0.808417	+14.00	String-to-Tree SMT
Online D	37	Other	YES	9.37	8.93	8.84	0.606905	0.606328	0.604149	-14.50	Online D
Online C	216	Other	YES	7.26	7.01	6.72	0.612808	0.613075	0.611563	—	Online C
RBMT B	243	RBMT	NO	17.86	17.75	17.49	0.744818	0.745885	0.743794	-20.00	RBMT B
RBMT C	244	RBMT	NO	9.62	9.96	9.59	0.642278	0.648758	0.645385	—	RBMT C
NAIST 1	122	SMT	NO	30.53	30.46	30.25	0.818040	0.819406	0.819492	+17.75	Travatar-based Forest-to-String SMT System
NAIST 2	123	SMT	NO	29.83	29.77	29.54	0.829627	0.830839	0.830529	+1.25	Travatar-based Forest-to-String SMT System (Tuned BLEU+RIBES)
Kyoto-U 3	18	EBMT	NO	26.69	26.48	26.30	0.796402	0.798084	0.798383	—	Our baseline system
Kyoto-U 1	257	EBMT	NO	27.21	27.02	26.83	0.791270	0.792166	0.790743	-0.75	Our new baseline system after several modifications
Kyoto-U 2	259	EBMT	NO	27.67	27.44	27.34	0.788321	0.789069	0.788206	-8.75	Our new baseline system after several modifications + 20-best parses, KN7, RNNLM reranking
BJTUNLP	224	SMT	NO	24.12	23.76	23.55	0.794834	0.796186	0.793054	-3.75	SMT
Sense 2	175	SMT	NO	27.92	28.03	27.67	0.793876	0.796589	0.797332	—	SMT
Sense 1	201	SMT	NO	23.09	22.94	23.04	0.779495	0.779502	0.780262	+10.00	Character based SMT
NICT	260	SMT	NO	27.98	28.18	27.84	0.806070	0.808684	0.807809	+6.50	Pre-reordering for phrase-based SMT (dependency parsing + manual rules)
TOSHIBA 2	236	RBMT	YES	19.28	18.93	18.82	0.764491	0.765346	0.763931	-5.25	RBMT system
TOSHIBA 1	238	SMT and RBMT	YES	27.42	26.82	26.79	0.804444	0.803302	0.803980	+0.75	RBMT with SPE(Statistical Post Editing) system
WASUIPS 1	371	SMT	NO	22.71	22.49	22.39	0.776323	0.777615	0.777327	—	Our baseline system (segmentation tools: urheen and mecab, moses: 1.0).
WASUIPS 2	373	SMT	YES	24.70	24.25	24.28	0.790030	0.790460	0.790898	—	Our baseline system + additional quasi-parallel corpus (segmentation tools: urheen and mecab, moses: 1.0).
WASUIPS 3	376	SMT	NO	25.44	25.04	24.98	0.794244	0.793945	0.794823	—	Our baseline system (segmentation tools: urheen and mecab, moses: 2.1.1).
WASUIPS 4	377	SMT	YES	25.60	25.10	25.07	0.794716	0.795786	0.795594	—	Our baseline system + additional quasi-parallel corpus segmentation tools: urheen and mecab, moses: 2.1.1).
WASUIPS 5	381	SMT	NO	22.01	21.81	21.61	0.767418	0.767414	0.766092	—	Our baseline system (segmentation tools: kytea, moses: 1.0).
WASUIPS 6	382	SMT	YES	22.20	22.02	21.91	0.771952	0.773341	0.772107	—	Our baseline system + additional quasi-parallel corpus (segmentation tools: kytea, moses: 1.0).
WASUIPS 7	385	SMT	NO	25.45	25.10	25.01	0.793819	0.793308	0.793029	—	Our baseline system (segmentation tools: kytea, moses: 2.1.1).
WASUIPS 8	386	SMT	YES	25.68	25.01	25.11	0.795721	0.795504	0.795129	—	Our baseline system + additional quasi-parallel corpus (segmentation tools: kytea, moses: 2.1.1).
WASUIPS 9	389	SMT	NO	25.08	24.81	24.64	0.790498	0.791430	0.790142	—	Our baseline system (segmentation tools: stanford-ctb and juman, moses: 2.1.1).
WASUIPS 10	390	SMT	YES	25.63	25.30	25.18	0.794646	0.795307	0.794024	—	Our baseline system + additional quasi-parallel corpus (segmentation tools: stanford-ctb and juman, moses: 2.1.1).

Table 13: JC submissions

SYSTEM ID	ID	METHOD	OTHER RESOURCES	BLEU			RIBES			HUMAN	SYSTEM DESCRIPTION
				juman	kytea	mecab	juman	kytea	mecab		
SMT Hiero	4	SMT	NO	35.43	35.91	35.64	0.810406	0.798726	0.807665	+4.75	Hierarchical Phrase-based SMT
SMT Phrase	8	SMT	NO	34.65	35.16	34.77	0.772498	0.766384	0.771005	—	Phrase-based SMT
SMT T2S	13	SMT	NO	36.52	37.07	36.64	0.825292	0.820490	0.825025	+16.00	Tree-to-String SMT
Online A	36	Other	YES	11.63	13.21	11.87	0.595925	0.598172	0.598573	-21.75	Online A
Online B	215	Other	YES	10.48	11.26	10.47	0.600733	0.596006	0.600706	—	Online B
RBMT A	239	RBMT	NO	9.37	9.87	9.35	0.666277	0.652402	0.661730	-37.75	RBMT A
RBMT D	242	RBMT	NO	8.39	8.70	8.30	0.641189	0.626400	0.633319	—	RBMT D
NAIST 1	120	SMT	NO	40.11	41.29	40.30	0.842477	0.834824	0.842235	+50.75	Travatar-based Forest-to-String SMT System
NAIST 2	124	SMT	NO	40.21	40.82	40.15	0.845486	0.838092	0.845625	+38.00	Travatar-based Forest-to-String SMT System (Tuned BLEU+RIBES)
EIWA 2	137	RBMT	YES	18.69	18.33	18.32	0.740183	0.720281	0.732466	—	RBMT plus user dictionary
EIWA 1	138	SMT and RBMT	YES	33.53	33.74	33.87	0.811350	0.800506	0.808504	+15.00	RBMT with user dictionary plus SPE(statistical post editing)
Kyoto-U 3	133	EBMT	NO	33.26	35.09	33.62	0.791680	0.787105	0.791269	—	Using n-best parses and RNNLM
Kyoto-U 4	135	EBMT	NO	32.68	33.30	32.45	0.786229	0.783016	0.786352	—	Our baseline system
Kyoto-U 2	258	EBMT	NO	33.57	34.43	33.45	0.800949	0.795390	0.800986	+6.00	Our new baseline system after several modifications
Kyoto-U 1	268	EBMT	NO	34.75	35.89	34.83	0.802629	0.798631	0.802930	+7.50	Our new baseline system after several modifications + 20-best parses, KN7, RNNLM reranking
SAS_MT 2	232	SMT	NO	36.58	36.22	36.10	0.822180	0.807535	0.817368	—	Syntactic reordering phrase-based SMT (SAS token tool)
SAS_MT 1	263	SMT	NO	37.42	37.65	37.07	0.834170	0.825551	0.833048	+22.50	Syntactic reordering Hierarchical SMT (using SAS token tool)
Sense 2	174	SMT	NO	34.56	35.08	34.64	0.771975	0.766470	0.771081	—	SMT
Sense 1	200	SMT	NO	33.66	33.86	33.46	0.789495	0.774338	0.784012	-1.00	Character based SMT
WASUIPS 1	369	SMT	NO	27.66	28.09	28.20	0.779183	0.762949	0.770846	—	Our baseline system (segmentation tools: urheen and mecab, moses: 1.0).
WASUIPS 2	370	SMT	YES	30.44	30.92	30.86	0.789824	0.773142	0.781475	—	Our baseline system + additional quasi-parallel corpus (segmentation tools: urheen and mecab, moses: 1.0).
WASUIPS 3	374	SMT	NO	31.87	32.26	32.26	0.794303	0.777876	0.786422	—	Our baseline system (segmentation tools: urheen and mecab, moses: 2.1.1).
WASUIPS 4	375	SMT	YES	32.19	32.55	32.54	0.795838	0.780027	0.787591	—	Our baseline system + additional quasi-parallel corpus (segmentation tools: urheen and mecab, moses: 2.1.1).
WASUIPS 5	379	SMT	NO	27.37	28.28	27.43	0.774423	0.753749	0.767073	—	Our baseline system (segmentation tools: kytea, moses: 1.0).
WASUIPS 6	380	SMT	YES	27.86	28.89	28.00	0.776550	0.756721	0.769409	—	Our baseline system + additional quasi-parallel corpus (segmentation tools: kytea, moses: 1.0).
WASUIPS 7	383	SMT	NO	32.08	33.09	32.18	0.793230	0.775168	0.787665	—	Our baseline system (segmentation tools: kytea, moses: 2.1.1).
WASUIPS 8	384	SMT	YES	32.43	33.36	32.48	0.796220	0.778075	0.789657	—	Our baseline system + additional quasi-parallel corpus (segmentation tools: kytea, moses: 2.1.1).
WASUIPS 9	387	SMT	NO	32.52	32.69	32.47	0.796059	0.780402	0.790107	—	Our baseline system (segmentation tools: stanford-ctb and juman, moses: 2.1.1).
WASUIPS 10	388	SMT	YES	32.65	32.81	32.59	0.796777	0.781733	0.791219	—	Our baseline system + additional quasi-parallel corpus (segmentation tools: stanford-ctb and juman, moses: 2.1.1).

Table 14: CJ submissions

References

Jingsheng Cai, Yujie Zhang, Hua Shan, and Jinan Xu. 2014. System Description: Dependency-based Preordering for Japanese-Chinese Machine Translation. In *Proceedings of the 1st Workshop on Asian Translation (WAT2014)*.

Chenchen Ding, Masao Utiyama, Eiichiro Sumita, and Mikio Yamamoto. 2014. Word Order Does NOT Differ Significantly Between Chinese and Japanese. In *Proceedings of the 1st Workshop on Asian Translation (WAT2014)*.

Terumasa Ehara. 2014. A machine translation system combining rule-based machine translation and statistical post-editing. In *Proceedings of the 1st Workshop on Asian Translation (WAT2014)*.

J.L. Fleiss et al. 1971. Measuring nominal scale agreement among many raters. *Psychological Bulletin*, 76(5):378–382.

Kenneth Heafield, Ivan Pouzyrevsky, Jonathan H. Clark, and Philipp Koehn. 2013. Scalable modified kneser-ney language model estimation. In *Proceedings of the 51st Annual Meeting of the Association for Computational Linguistics (Volume 2: Short Papers)*, pages 690–696, Sofia, Bulgaria, August. Association for Computational Linguistics.

Hieu Hoang, Philipp Koehn, and Adam Lopez. 2009. A unified framework for phrase-based, hierarchical, and syntax-based statistical machine translation. In *Proceedings of the International Workshop on Spoken Language Translation*, pages 152–159.

Sho Hoshino, Hubert Soyer, Yusuke Miyao, and Akiko Aizawa. 2014. Japanese to English Machine Translation using Preordering and Compositional Distributed Semantics. In *Proceedings of the 1st Workshop on Asian Translation (WAT2014)*.

Hideki Isozaki, Tsutomu Hirao, Kevin Duh, Katsuhito Sudoh, and Hajime Tsukada. 2010. Automatic evaluation of translation quality for distant language pairs. In *Proceedings of the 2010 Conference on Empirical Methods in Natural Language Processing*, EMNLP '10, pages 944–952, Stroudsburg, PA, USA. Association for Computational Linguistics.

Philipp Koehn, Hieu Hoang, Alexandra Birch, Chris Callison-Burch, Marcello Federico, Nicola Bertoldi, Brooke Cowan, Wade Shen, Christine Moran, Richard Zens, Chris Dyer, Ondrej Bojar, Alexandra Constantin, and Evan Herbst. 2007. Moses: Open source toolkit for statistical machine translation. In *Annual Meeting of the Association for Computational Linguistics (ACL), demonstration session*.

Philipp Koehn. 2004. Statistical significance tests for machine translation evaluation. In Dekang Lin and Dekai Wu, editors, *Proceedings of EMNLP 2004*, pages 388–395, Barcelona, Spain, July. Association for Computational Linguistics.

T. Kudo. 2005. Mecab : Yet another part-of-speech and morphological analyzer. *http://mecab.sourceforge.net/*.

Sadao Kurohashi, Toshihisa Nakamura, Yuji Matsumoto, and Makoto Nagao. 1994. Improvements of Japanese morphological analyzer JUMAN. In *Proceedings of The International Workshop on Sharable Natural Language*, pages 22–28.

Graham Neubig, Yosuke Nakata, and Shinsuke Mori. 2011. Pointwise prediction for robust, adaptable japanese morphological analysis. In *Proceedings of the 49th Annual Meeting of the Association for Computational Linguistics: Human Language Technologies: Short Papers - Volume 2*, HLT '11, pages 529–533, Stroudsburg, PA, USA. Association for Computational Linguistics.

Graham Neubig. 2014. Forest-to-String SMT for Asian Language Translation: NAIST at WAT 2014. In *Proceedings of the 1st Workshop on Asian Translation (WAT2014)*.

Kenichi Ohwada, Ryosuke Miyazaki, and Mamoru Komachi. 2014. Predicate-Argument Structure-based Preordering for Japanese-English Statistical Machine Translation of Scientific Papers. In *Proceedings of the 1st Workshop on Asian Translation (WAT2014)*.

Kishore Papineni, Salim Roukos, Todd Ward, and Wei-Jing Zhu. 2002. Bleu: a method for automatic evaluation of machine translation. In *ACL*, pages 311–318.

Slav Petrov, Leon Barrett, Romain Thibaux, and Dan Klein. 2006. Learning accurate, compact, and interpretable tree annotation. In *Proceedings of the 21st International Conference on Computational Linguistics and 44th Annual Meeting of the Association for Computational Linguistics*, pages 433–440, Sydney, Australia, July. Association for Computational Linguistics.

John Richardson, Fabien Cromières, Toshiaki Nakazawa, and Sadao Kurohashi. 2014. KyotoEBMT System Description for the 1st Workshop on Asian Translation. In *Proceedings of the 1st Workshop on Asian Translation (WAT2014)*.

Satoshi Sonoh, Satoshi Kinoshita, Hiroyuki Tanaka, and Satoshi Kamatani. 2014. Toshiba MT System Description for the WAT2014 Workshop. In *Proceedings of the 1st Workshop on Asian Translation (WAT2014)*.

Liling Tan and Francis Bond. 2014. Manipulating Input Data in Machine Translation. In *Proceedings of the 1st Workshop on Asian Translation (WAT2014)*.

Huihsin Tseng. 2005. A conditional random field word segmenter. In *In Fourth SIGHAN Workshop on Chinese Language Processing*.

Masao Utiyama and Hitoshi Isahara. 2007. A japanese-english patent parallel corpus. In *MT summit XI*, pages 475–482.

Rui Wang, Xu Yang, and Yan Gao. 2014. The SAS Statistical Machine Translation System for WAT 2014. In *Proceedings of the 1st Workshop on Asian Translation (WAT2014)*.

Wei Yang and Yves Lepage. 2014. Consistent Improvement in Translation Quality of Chinese–Japanese Technical Texts by Adding Additional Quasi-parallel Training Data. In *Proceedings of the 1st Workshop on Asian Translation (WAT2014)*.

Zhongyuan Zhu. 2014. Weblio Pre-reordering Statistical Machine Translation System. In *Proceedings of the 1st Workshop on Asian Translation (WAT2014)*.

Forest-to-String SMT for Asian Language Translation: NAIST at WAT 2014

Graham Neubig
Graduate School of Information Science
Nara Institute of Science and Technology
8916-5 Takayama-cho, Ikoma-shi, Nara, Japan
neubig@is.naist.jp

Abstract

This paper describes the Nara Institute of Science and Technology's (NAIST) submission to the 2014 Workshop on Asian Translation's four translation tasks. All systems are based on forest-to-string (F2S) translation, in which the input sentence is first parsed using a syntactic parser, then a forest of possible syntactic analyses is translated into the target language. In addition to the baseline F2S system, we add rescoring using a recurrent neural network language model (RNNLM), which allows for more fluent output. The resulting system achieved the highest results in both automatic and manual evaluation for all four of the language pairs targeted by the workshop.

1 Introduction

The Workshop on Asian Translation (WAT) 2014 (Nakazawa et al., 2014) included a translation task over four language pairs, all involving translating Japanese (ja), a language with SOV word order, to/from English (en) or Chinese (zh), languages with SVO word order. Because of this, it can be expected that one of the major challenges facing translation systems in this task is the proper reordering of the words between the source and target languages.

One promising way to tackle the reordering problem is through the use of tree-to-string (T2S) translation, a translation formalism where the source sentence is first parsed using a syntactic parser, then sub-structures of the parse tree are translated into target-side strings (Liu et al., 2006). Mi et al. (2008) have also demonstrated that forest-to-string (F2S) translation allows for more robust use of source-side syntax by not considering a 1-best parse tree, but a myriad of parse candidates stored efficiently in a packed-forest data structure. In our previous work (Neubig and Duh, 2014), we have shown that F2S translation is effective for en-ja and ja-en translation, and can outperform alternative methods such as pre- or post-ordering. Thus, in our WAT submission, we choose this formalism, and specifically it's implementation in the open-source Travatar decoder[1] (Neubig, 2013) as the base of our system.

Another promising development over the past couple years is the use of continuous-space representations of language combined with neural-network-based probabilistic models. These have been incorporated into translation as either language models (LMs) (Vaswani et al., 2013) or translation models (TMs) (Le et al., 2012), allowing for large increases in translation accuracy. In our submission, we incorporate this continuous-space representation by training a recurrent neural network language model (RNNLM; Mikolov et al. (2010)) and using its scores as a feature in n-best hypothesis rescoring.

We also made a few small improvements to our ja-en system, mainly in an attempt to reduce the number of unknown words. Specifically, we perform compound splitting (Koehn and Knight, 2003) of unknown words to help reduce the effects of under-segmentation, perform one small word substitution to regularize for the peculiarities of the development/test data, and add large external dictionaries.

As a result of the incorporation of F2S translation and RNNLMs, we see a large gain in accuracy over a baseline phrase-based machine translation model. Specifically, we see a gain in BLEU of 8.21 for en-ja, 5.44 for ja-en, 4.71 for zh-ja, and 2.47 for ja-zh. In addition, according to the official automatic evaluation, our system outperformed all other submitted systems in all tracks. Scripts to

[1] http://phontron.com/travatar

Proceedings of the 1st Workshop on Asian Translation (WAT2014), pages 20–25,
Tokyo, Japan, 4th October 2014.

largely reproduce our experiments will be released open source.[2]

2 Data and Data Processing

2.1 Data Used

For the majority of our systems, we simply used the ASPEC corpus provided by the WAT task. For the zh-ja and ja-zh systems, we used all of the data, amounting to 672k sentences. For the en-ja and ja-en systems, we used all of the data for training the language models, but because the ja-en translation data was automatically aligned and low-confidence sentences were often noisy, we only used the first 2 million sentences of the training data, discarding the rest.

In addition to this official data, for the ja-en pair we submitted one system that used additional dictionaries to reduce the number of unknown words. Specifically, we used the EDICT[3], and Eijiro[4] dictionaries, as well as the Japanese-English links between Wikipedia pages. There are a number of ways to incorporate these dictionaries, but in the submitted system, we simply added a rule to the translation table for all unknown words that existed in the dictionary.

2.2 Tokenization and Preprocessing

For English, Japanese, and Chinese, tokenization was performed using the Stanford Parser (Klein and Manning, 2003), the KyTea toolkit (Neubig et al., 2011), and the Stanford Segmenter (Tseng et al., 2005) respectively. We also performed case normalization for English, by changing the first word in English sentences to its most common capitalization before training models and translation, and capitalizing the first letter of the sentence after translation.[5] For zh-ja translation, in order to make unknown words more comprehensible, we converted simplified Chinese characters to their Japanese equivalents, and vice-versa for ja-zh translation (using the `Kanconvit.pm` Perl script).

In addition to our standard tokenization, for Japanese, while KyTea is on average more robust to unknown words than other standard alternative word segmenters for Japanese, it also has a greater tendency to under-segment words, which can be detrimental for machine translation. As a quick fix to this problem, we re-segmented all words that appear in the dev or test set but not the training set using the compound segmentation method of (Koehn and Knight, 2003), which splits words into two, resolving ambiguities such that the newly split words have the highest unigram probability.

Finally, in a preliminary analysis of our ja-en system using the error analysis method of Akabe et al. (2014),[6] we discovered a peculiarity in the development data: prolific use of the word "標題" (which can be translated into "the mentioned," or "the XX in the title"). This word appeared prolifically in the dev set (as well as devtest and test), but not once in the training corpus. In order to solve this problem, we normalized "標題" into the lexically different but semantically largely equivalent "表題," which appeared many times in the training corpus.

2.3 Syntactic Parsing

As we are performing translation using syntactic parsing, it is essential that we have an accurate syntactic parser. Based on the experiments presented in Neubig and Duh (2014) we opt to use the Egret parser,[7] which implements the latent variable parsing model of (Petrov et al., 2006).

For the parsing models in English and Chinese, we use models trained on the English and Chinese Penn Treebanks respectively (Marcus et al., 1993; Xue et al., 2005). For the Japanese model, we train our own model on the Japanese Word Dependency Treebank (Mori et al., 2014). As this is a dependency treebank, we use head rules contained the Travatar toolkit to transform the dependency trees into phrase structure trees.[8]

For training, we simply use 1-best parses, but at test time we use a forest of parse trees, specifically using forests with all tree edges that exist in at least one of the 100-best parses.

3 Model Training

3.1 Alignment

For T2S translation, it is necessary to have an accurate word alignment model, which allows for the extraction of more rules that match the parse tree, and the estimation of more accurate reordering probabilities (Neubig and Duh, 2014).

[2] `http://phontron.com/project/wat2014`

[3] `http://www.edrdg.org/jmdict/edict.html`

[4] `http://www.eijiro.jp`

[5] This is often referred to as "truecasing."

[6] In fact we slightly modified the method to use the translation reference and a smoothed naive Bayes classifier.

[7] `https://github.com/neubig/egret`

[8] `ja-depadjust.pl` and `ja-dep2cfg.pl`

Thus, for en-ja and ja-en translation, we use Nile[9] (Riesa and Marcu, 2010), a supervised syntax-based aligner that can improve alignment accuracy by incorporating information about parse trees and learn from manually created alignments. For our manual alignments, we use the alignments provided by the Kyoto Free Translation Task (Neubig, 2011). Unfortunately, for zh-ja and ja-zh translation, we do not have any hand-aligned data available, so we use the GIZA++ unsupervised aligner (Och and Ney, 2003).

3.2 Translation Model Training

For training our translation model, we extract a synchronous tree substitution grammar (STSG) according to the method of Galley et al. (2006). We used composed rules including up to 5 minimal rules, and attached null-aligned words to the highest possible point in the parse tree. For the translation model features, we used a standard set of 5 features including forward and backward translation probabilities, forward and backward lexical probabilities, and the phrase penalty. When calculating the translation probabilities, we first applied Kneser-Ney smoothing to the phrases counts (Kneser and Ney, 1995).

3.3 Language Model Training

For all systems, we trained a 6-gram language model smoothed with modified Kneser-Ney smoothing using KenLM (Heafield et al., 2013). In addition, because we had two different data sets containing Japanese data (en-ja and zh-ja), we trained two separate language models and interpolated them together. We chose different interpolation coefficients for the en-ja and zh-ja tasks by choosing the interpolation coefficients that maximize the likelihood on the development data on each of the respective tasks. This gave us a small but significant improvement in perplexity on the development set.

In addition to the n-gram language model, we incorporated a recurrent neural network language model (RNNLM) (Mikolov et al., 2010). This, as mentioned in the introduction, will allow us to incorporate recent advances in continuous-space language modeling, improving robustness to unknown or low-frequency linguistic phenomena. We used the RNNLM toolkit,[10] with 500 hidden layers and 300 classes. Because training RNNLM on large data sets is prohibitively expensive, we used only the first 500,000 sentences from the parallel data to train models for each respective task. As RNNLMs cannot be trivially incorporated into decoding due to their continuous-space state representation, we instead use the RNNLM score as an additional feature in 10,000-best rescoring of the output of the baseline model.

[9] `https://code.google.com/p/nile/`

[10] `http://rnnlm.org`

3.4 Parameter Optimization

In order to optimize the parameters of the log-linear model, we use standard minimum error rate training (MERT; Och (2003)). As the two official evaluation measures of the contest are BLEU (Papineni et al., 2002) and RIBES (Isozaki et al., 2010), we submitted two systems, one optimized for BLEU, and one optimized for BLEU+RIBES. We also attempted optimizing for RIBES only, which did result in higher RIBES scores, but also extremely short translations and extremely low scores, so we decided against submitting this system.

4 Issues for Context-aware Machine Translation

We did not make any particular attempt to consider super-sentential context in our system. Sub-sentential context is considered to a lesser extent by the n-gram LM, and to a greater extent by the RNNLM, the theoretically infinite history of which could potentially capture syntactic or semantic agreement of words that are beyond the scope of traditional n-grams.

5 Experimental Results

In Table 1 we show the results for our systems with and without the RNNLM, and tuning with BLEU or BLEU+RIBES. In addition, we show the results for a PBMT system trained using the Moses toolkit (Koehn et al., 2007), with the same data as the F2S system and the default settings except for a reordering limit of 18, which gave better results on all language pairs than the default of 6.

From this table we can first see that the F2S translation greatly outperforms PBMT. The trend is more prominent in the translation to or from English, a result of the fact that the amount of reordering is greater between English and Japanese than between Chinese and Japanese. In addition, we can see that the gain over PBMT is smaller

System	RNN	Tune	en-ja		ja-en		zh-ja		ja-zh	
			B	R	B	R	B	R	B	R
PBMT	No	B	29.00	68.99	19.41	64.71	35.57	76.78	27.07	79.80
F2S	No	B	36.50	79.69	23.76	71.79	39.82	82.42	29.27	81.26
		B+R	36.24	79.95	24.02	71.77	39.22	83.10	28.83	82.58
	Yes	B	**37.21**	80.21	24.72	72.39	**40.61**	83.18	**29.78**	81.66
		B+R	**36.94**	**80.78**	**25.12**	**72.64**	40.01	**83.52**	29.03	**82.82**
F2S+Dict	Yes	B	-		**25.27**	**72.56**	-		-	

Table 1: Overall BLEU and RIBES results for a baseline Moses, and five of our systems without and with the RNNLM rescoring, tuning for BLEU or BLEU+RIBES, and with/without dictionaries. Bold indicates systems not statistically different from the best system according to bootstrap resampling (Koehn, 2004).

in pairs where the source is Japanese. We account this to the fact that the syntactic parsing accuracy is lower, partly due to the fact that the training data for the parser is smaller (approximately 6,000 sentences), and partly due to the fact that we have done very little grammar engineering for Japanese, in contrast to the more carefully thought-out phrase structure of the English and Chinese treebanks.

Next, taking a look at the results with RNNLM, we can see that adding RNNLM helps across all language pairs on the order of 0.7-1.0 BLEU points, with slightly smaller gains for RIBES. These consistent gains are in concert with previous results, adding further evidence to the observation that continuous space language models are beneficial for translation.

We can also see that adding RIBES to the evaluation function used in parameter optimization leads to a significant increase in RIBES across all data sets. On the other hand, it also leads to a decrease in BLEU for the ja-zh and zh-ja data sets, although no significant decrease is observed in the ja-en and en-ja data sets.

It should also be noted that the systems tuned for BLEU+RIBES tend to result in significantly shorter translation outputs than other systems. Table 2 shows the average length of sentences for each of the systems (using RNNLM in all cases). From this, we can see that for all language pairs except ja-en, BLEU-tuned systems tend to largely match the length of the reference hypotheses, while the BLEU+RIBES tuned systems are significantly shorter.

Tune	en-ja	ja-en	zh-ja	ja-zh
B	29.86	25.10	37.26	27.55
B+R	28.40	25.05	35.61	25.64
Ref.	29.73	24.39	37.51	27.78

Table 2: The average number of words per sentence according to different tuning objectives, as well as for the reference.

6 Official Results

In this section, we discuss the official results of the evaluation focusing on two aspects: the relationship with human evaluation, and a comparison with other systems. In Table 3 we show the official results for each system, including human evaluation. When reports for multiple segmenters are reported, we display the ones calculated using KyTea. Human evaluation is calculated according to pairwise comparison with the baseline according to the official task description (Nakazawa et al., 2014), where 100 indicates that the proposed system exceeds the baseline in all judgements, and 0 indicates that the system is equivalent with the baseline.

First, we note that the NAIST submissions achieved the highest score in all three evaluation measures across all four language pairs. The competing teams include PBMT, Hiero, tree-to-string, string-to-tree systems prepared by the organizers, as well as systems prepared by the participants (often based on preordering, or statistical post-editing of rule-based MT). This provides further evidence to support our previous observation that F2S translation provides strong results for the language pairs under consideration for the WAT task (Neubig and Duh, 2014).

		en-ja			ja-en			zh-ja			ja-zh		
Dict	Tune	B	R	H	B	R	H	B	R	H	B	R	H
No	B	**37.2**	80.2	**56.3**	23.3	**72.4**	**37.5**	**41.3**	83.5	**50.8**	**30.5**	81.8	**17.8**
	B+R	**37.2**	**80.7**	**51.5**	23.5	**72.4**	-	40.8	**83.8**	38.0	29.8	**83.0**	1.3
Yes	B		-		**23.8**	**72.3**	**40.5**		-			-	
Best B		35.0	79.0	36.0	21.1	69.9	25.0	37.7	82.6	22.5	28.7	81.0	**14.0**
Best R		35.0	79.0	36.0	20.6	70.8	23.3	37.7	82.6	22.5	27.7	81.0	3.8
Best H		34.9	78.6	43.3	20.4	67.8	25.5	37.7	82.6	22.5	28.7	81.0	**14.0**

Table 3: BLEU, RIBES, and HUMAN evaluation according to the official evaluation results. We also show the best competing systems other than ours according to each evaluation metric. Bold indicates systems within 0.3 of the best system for BLEU and RIBES, and systems that do not show a significant decrease from the best system according to Student's t-test for HUMAN ($p < 0.05$).

System	Translation
Source	由于气候变化和能源保障问题，引入了环境污染税和碳税，这对电力产业尤为重要。
Tuned B	気候の変化とエネルギー保障問題，環境汚染税と炭素税を導入し，電力産業に対して極めて重要である。
Tuned B+R	気候変化やエネルギー保障問題，環境汚染税と炭素税を導入し，電力産業が重要である。

Table 4: Examples of zh-ja translations for systems tuned with different objectives.

Next, we take a look at the correlation between automatic evaluation measures and human evaluation scores. Just looking at our systems, we can see that in general BLEU scores are a good indicator of human evaluation, while in many instances systems with higher RIBES scores achieve lower human evaluation. This is in contrary to previous evaluation campaigns including the Japanese language (Goto et al., 2011), and thus a somewhat noteworthy result.

We hypothesize that this is due to the fact, as mentioned in the previous section, that systems tuned for BLEU+RIBES achieve higher RIBES scores, but also produce short hypotheses. Because the hypotheses are short, they have a larger chance of dropping words and missing important information. We show one example of this in Table 4, where the BLEU system received a higher manual evaluation score than the BLEU+RIBES system. In this example, the system tuned with only BLEU produces a longer hypothesis than that of the system tuned with BLEU+RIBES. In particular, focusing on the word "に対して" ("for" in English), the BLEU system includes this word and is able to achieve a translation corresponding to the true meaning of "is important for the electric industry," while the BLEU+RIBES system drops the word, causing a mistaken translation of "the electric industry is important."

7 Conclusion

In this paper we described the NAIST submission to the WAT 2014 translation task. The system was based on forest-to-string statistical machine translation, and achieved the highest translation accuracy on all four language pairs.

While the accuracy was relatively high, there is still significant amounts of work to be done. First, our subjective assessment of the translation results indicated that the parsing accuracy for Japanese is still likely lower than it is for other languages. Examining the use of other, more accurate parsers for Japanese is high on the list of priorities. In addition, the statistical model used in our translation system is a standard one based on standard maximum likelihood estimation and minimum error rate training of a small number of dense features. In future work we hope to improve both the model estimation and parameter tuning processes using more sophisticated models, features, and methods.

Acknowledgments:

This work was supported by JSPS KAKENHI Grant Number 25730136.

References

Koichi Akabe, Graham Neubig, Sakriani Sakti, Tomoki Toda, and Satoshi Nakamura. 2014. Discriminative language models as a tool for machine translation error analysis. In *Proc. COLING*, pages 1124–1132.

Michel Galley, Jonathan Graehl, Kevin Knight, Daniel Marcu, Steve DeNeefe, Wei Wang, and Ignacio Thayer. 2006. Scalable inference and training of context-rich syntactic translation models. In *Proc. ACL*, pages 961–968.

Isao Goto, Bin Lu, Ka Po Chow, Eiichiro Sumita, and Benjamin K. Tsou. 2011. Overview of the patent machine translation task at the NTCIR-9 workshop. In *Proceedings of NTCIR*, volume 9, pages 559–578.

Kenneth Heafield, Ivan Pouzyrevsky, Jonathan H. Clark, and Philipp Koehn. 2013. Scalable modified Kneser-Ney language model estimation. In *Proc. ACL*, pages 690–696.

Hideki Isozaki, Tsutomu Hirao, Kevin Duh, Katsuhito Sudoh, and Hajime Tsukada. 2010. Automatic evaluation of translation quality for distant language pairs. In *Proc. EMNLP*, pages 944–952.

Dan Klein and Christopher D. Manning. 2003. Accurate unlexicalized parsing. In *Proc. ACL*, pages 423–430.

Reinhard Kneser and Hermann Ney. 1995. Improved backing-off for M-gram language modeling. *Proc. ICASSP*.

Philipp Koehn and Kevin Knight. 2003. Empirical methods for compound splitting. In *Proc. EACL*.

Philipp Koehn, Hieu Hoang, Alexandra Birch, Chris Callison-Burch, Marcello Federico, Nicola Bertoldi, Brooke Cowan, Wade Shen, Christine Moran, Richard Zens, Chris Dyer, Ondrej Bojar, Alexandra Constantin, and Evan Herbst. 2007. Moses: Open source toolkit for statistical machine translation. In *Proc. ACL*, pages 177–180.

Philipp Koehn. 2004. Statistical significance tests for machine translation evaluation. In *Proc. EMNLP*.

Hai-Son Le, Alexandre Allauzen, and François Yvon. 2012. Continuous space translation models with neural networks. In *Proc. NAACL*, pages 39–48.

Yang Liu, Qun Liu, and Shouxun Lin. 2006. Tree-to-string alignment template for statistical machine translation. In *Proc. ACL*.

Mitchell P Marcus, Mary Ann Marcinkiewicz, and Beatrice Santorini. 1993. Building a large annotated corpus of English: The Penn treebank. *Computational linguistics*, 19(2):313–330.

Haitao Mi, Liang Huang, and Qun Liu. 2008. Forest-based translation. In *Proc. ACL*, pages 192–199.

Tomas Mikolov, Martin Karafiát, Lukas Burget, Jan Cernockỳ, and Sanjeev Khudanpur. 2010. Recurrent neural network based language model. In *Proc. 11th InterSpeech*, pages 1045–1048.

Shinsuke Mori, Hideki Ogura, and Tetsuro Sasada. 2014. A Japanese word dependency corpus. In *Proc. LREC*.

Toshiaki Nakazawa, Hideki Mino, Isao Goto, Sadao Kurohashi, and Eiichiro Sumita. 2014. Overview of the 1st Workshop on Asian Translation. In *Proc. WAT*.

Graham Neubig and Kevin Duh. 2014. On the elements of an accurate tree-to-string machine translation system. In *Proc. ACL*.

Graham Neubig, Yosuke Nakata, and Shinsuke Mori. 2011. Pointwise prediction for robust, adaptable Japanese morphological analysis. In *Proc. ACL*, pages 529–533.

Graham Neubig. 2011. The Kyoto free translation task. `http://www.phontron.com/kftt`.

Graham Neubig. 2013. Travatar: A forest-to-string machine translation engine based on tree transducers. In *Proc. ACL Demo Track*, pages 91–96.

Franz Josef Och and Hermann Ney. 2003. A systematic comparison of various statistical alignment models. *Computational Linguistics*, 29(1):19–51.

Franz Josef Och. 2003. Minimum error rate training in statistical machine translation. In *Proc. ACL*, pages 160–167.

Kishore Papineni, Salim Roukos, Todd Ward, and Wei-Jing Zhu. 2002. BLEU: a method for automatic evaluation of machine translation. In *Proc. ACL*, pages 311–318.

Slav Petrov, Leon Barrett, Romain Thibaux, and Dan Klein. 2006. Learning accurate, compact, and interpretable tree annotation. In *Proc. ACL*, pages 433–440.

Jason Riesa and Daniel Marcu. 2010. Hierarchical search for word alignment. In *Proc. ACL*, pages 157–166.

Huihsin Tseng, Pichuan Chang, Galen Andrew, Daniel Jurafsky, and Christopher Manning. 2005. A conditional random field word segmenter for sighan bakeoff 2005. In *Proc. SIGHAN*.

Ashish Vaswani, Yinggong Zhao, Victoria Fossum, and David Chiang. 2013. Decoding with large-scale neural language models improves translation. In *Proc. EMNLP*, pages 1387–1392.

Naiwen Xue, Fei Xia, Fu-Dong Chiou, and Martha Palmer. 2005. The Penn Chinese treebank: Phrase structure annotation of a large corpus. *Natural language engineering*, 11(02):207–238.

Toshiba MT System Description for the WAT2014 Workshop

Satoshi Sonoh, Satoshi Kinoshita, Hiroyuki Tanaka and Satoshi Kamatani

Knowledge Media Laboratory, Corporate Research & Development Center,
Toshiba Corporation.
1, Komukai Toshiba-cho, Saiwai-ku, Kawasaki 212-8582, JAPAN
satoshi.sonoo@toshiba.co.jp

Abstract

This paper provides a system description of Toshiba Machine Translation System for WAT2014. We participated in two tasks, namely Japanese-English translation and Japanese-Chinese translation. In each task, we submitted two results; one is a result of a rule-based translation system, and the other is a result which is an output of statistical post editing trained with the ASPEC training corpora. In both tasks, output by statistical post editing shows improvement in machine evaluation, but we obtained different results from human evaluation.

1 Introduction

Toshiba has been developing a Rule-Based Machine Translation (RBMT) system. Recently, open parallel corpora such as ASPEC[1] are available for development of machine translation systems. However, it is extremely high cost to develop a large volume of parallel corpora in wide-domain for commercial use. For this reason, we have developed translation functions by using a monolingual corpus in the target language in order to improve performance. For example, a target word selection is possible based on co-occurrence relationship extracted from a monolingual corpus (Suzuki and Kumano, 2005). Moreover, we tackled a domain adaptation by using a parallel corpus and proposed a system which consists of RBMT and statistical post editing (SPE) (Suzuki, 2011). Furthermore, we have developed a word sense disambiguation based on a monolingual corpus in the target domain, and it has been applied to Japanese-Korean/Korean-Japanese translation system (Kumano, 2012).

In this evaluation task, we submitted two types of results for each Japanese-English translation and Japanese-Chinese translation (Nakazawa et al., 2014). One is our RBMT system which is developed for translating open domain written texts. The other is a combination of RBMT and SPE which is trained by the target domain corpus.

Section 2 describes the overview of our system. The preparation and results for the task are shown in Section 3 and 4. A context-aware translation is discussed in Section 5. Finally, Section 6 concludes this paper.

2 Overview of Toshiba System

2.1 Baseline System

Our system realizes transfer-based machine translation (Izuha et al., 2008). The core framework consists of morphological analysis, syntactic/semantic analysis, target word selection, structural transfer, syntactic generation and morphological generation. Furthermore, huge amount of rules as translation knowledge including word dictionaries can realize both high translation performance and flexibility of customization.

2.2 Statistical Post Editing

Although RBMT may preserve a certain level of adequacy in expected domain such as a manual document, translation knowledge for target word selection is not enough for a specific domain. Moreover, fluency for RBMT output is typically low in comparison with Statistical Machine Translation (SMT).

Statistical post editing by using phrase-based SMT has been proposed and it is an efficient method which is able to adapt translation output to the target domain (Simard et al., 2007). The combination of RBMT and SPE has the potential to improve the translation quality without additional rules (Simard et al., 2007).

[1] http://lotus.kuee.kyoto-u.ac.jp/ASPEC/

Proceedings of the 1st Workshop on Asian Translation (WAT2014), pages 26–32,
Tokyo, Japan, 4th October 2014.

In the evaluation task, we realized SPE based on phrase-based SMT (Kohen et al., 2003) by using the training corpus (1.0M sentences for English, 0.67M for Chinese) and its translation output by our RBMT system. We used Moses tools (Kohen et al., 2007) for English tokenization, and Kytea (Neubig et al., 2011) for Chinese.

3 Preparation for the Task

3.1 Selecting Technical Term Dictionaries

As a preparation for the evaluation task, we selected technical term dictionaries which improve the baseline system. Toshiba provides customers with technical term dictionaries so that they can get better translation in their target domains. Table 1 shows a list of technical term dictionaries, which contain about 3 million words and 460 thousand words in total for Japanese-English and Japanese-Chinese translation systems respectively. But using all the available dictionaries does not necessarily lead to better translations because even a technical term for one domain should be translated differently in another domain.

To choose the best dictionary sets, we conducted two-step evaluation using the devset of ASPEC corpus. The first step is to find which technical term dictionary is useful or not by comparing the BLEU score with that of the baseline system[2]. The second step is to decide the best combination of dictionaries which are judged useful in the first step by adding them to the baseline system one by one as long as the addition gives a higher BLEU score.

In Japanese-English translation, 10 out of 18 technical term dictionaries provide better translations than the baseline system as shown in Table 2(a). In the second step, we started from adding two dictionaries, "namely Chemistry" and "Medicine/Pharmacology 2", and found that adding 4 technical dictionaries gave the best BLEU score as shown in Table 2(b).

In Japanese-Chinese translation, the first step showed that only two dictionaries provided better translations than the baseline system. We confirmed that this combination provides better result than those obtained in the previous step as shown in Table 2(c) and (d).

[2]The baseline system used technical dictionaries ("Proper noun" and "Internet") as default setting. For Japanese-English, "Natural/Social Sciences" is also used because the target domain is scientific papers.

JE	JC	dictionary name
x	-	Architecture/Civil Engineering
x	x	Auto
x	x	Biology
x	x	Business
x	x	Chemistry
x	x	Electricity/Electronics
x	x	Finance/Law
x	x	Industrial Technology
x	x	Information/Telecommunication
x	x	Internet
x	-	Japanese Scientific Terms
x	-	JIS Terms
x	-	Math/Physics
x	x	Mechanics
x	-	Medicine (Basic/Clinical)
x	-	Medicine/Pharmacology (Regulatory terms)
x	x	Medicine/Pharmacology 1
x	x	Medicine/Pharmacology 2
x	-	Military/Defense
x	-	Natural Science
x	-	Natural/Social Sciences
x	-	Nichigai/ Science and Technology (Basic Scicnce)
x	-	Nichigai/Medicine (Basic)
x	-	Nichigai/Medicine (Related fields)
x	-	Nichigai/Science and Technology (Engineering)
x	-	Nichigai/Science and Technology (Science/Medicine)
x	-	Nuclear Studies
x	-	Production/Quality
x	x	Proper Nouns (standard)
x	-	Proper Nouns (technical)
x	-	Textile/Garment
x	x	Transportation/Logistics

Table 1: List of technical term dictionaries.

ID	dictionary name	BLUE
1	Chemistry	16.04
2	Medicine/Pharmacology 2	15.95
3	Nichigai/Science and Technology (Science/Medicine)	15.93
4	Medicine (Basic/Clinical)	15.92
5	Natural/Social Sciences	15.89
6	Nichigai/Medicine (Basic)	15.88
7	Biology	15.88
8	Math/Physics	15.85
9	Information/Telecommunication	15.84
10	Nichigai/Medicine (Related fields)	15.81
	Baseline	15.47

(a) Result of step 1 for JE

dictionary ID	BLUE
1+2	16.11
1+2+3	16.15
1+2+3+4	**16.21**

(b) Result of step 2 for JE

ID	dictionary name	BLUE
1	Chemistry	18.89
2	Biology	18.86
	Baseline	18.73

(c) Result of step 1 for JC

dictionary ID	BLUE
1+2	**18.92**

(d) Result of step 2 for JC

Table 2: BLEU scores after adding technical term dictionaries.

3.2 Building Additional Dictionaries

To improve the performance of the baseline system, we have built additional dictionaries for Japanese-Chinese system by using the given training data. We first built a SMT system by using the standard Moses system, and extracted word pairs whose co-occurrence ratio is more than 0.7 from the phrase table. By using sentence pairs in the training corpus, we got about 10,000 word pairs as dictionary entry candidates. After filtering noisy results, we checked them manually and got about 5,400 terms for this task. By using this dictionary additionally, BLEU score for the development data was improved from 18.92 to 18.98. For Japanese-English system, we have built no additional dictionary.

Because the effect of the additional dictionary was little, finally, we used only selected technical dictionaries, and not use the additional dictionary.

4 Results

This section shows the evaluation results of our systems. We analyzed the relationship between machine evaluation and human evaluation. In addition to the human evaluation provided by WAT 2014, we evaluated the output by relative ranking of 1(best) to 3(worse) for the three systems including RBMT, RBMT with SPE and phrase-based SMT.

4.1 Japanese-English results

Table 3 summarizes the evaluation results of Japanese-English translation systems. In the machine evaluation, BLUE score for our tuned RBMT is 15.69 and 20.61 for RBMT with SPE, respectively. Adopting SPE achieved an improvement of 31.4% in BLUE score.

System	BLUE	RIBES	HUMAN	RANK
RBMT	15.69	0.69	20.25	**1.38**
+SPE	**20.61**	**0.71**	**23.25**	1.45
SMT	18.45	0.65	-	2.24

Table 3: Japanese-English evaluation results.

In the human evaluation, HUMAN score for RBMT with SPE is 3 points higher than RBMT. However, RANK score, which is the average ranks of 200 setences in testset (not same as HUMAN-set), shows a different result from crowdsourcing evaluation. In this regard, we have found out the differences between RBMT and RBMT with SPE as shown in Table 4. Although SPE surely achieved improvements of target word selection, there are some mistranslations such as deletion of word and disagreement of tense in SPE output. As a result, RBMT may get a better result than RBMT with SPE in the RANK evaluation.

4.2 Japanese-Chinese results

Table 4 summarizes the evaluation results of Japanese-Chinese translation systems. In Japanese-Chinese, BLUE score for our tuned RBMT is 19.28 and 27.42 for RBMT with SPE, respectively. A ratio of improvement is larger than JE results, and is 42.2%.

In the human evaluation, both HUMAN and RANK scores show that RBMT with SPE performs better than RBMT. Although results are

System	BLUE	RIBES	HUMAN	RANK
RBMT	19.28	0.76	-5.25	2.13
+SPE	27.42	0.80	**0.75**	1.76
SMT	**27.96**	0.79	-	**1.63**

Table 4: Japanese-Chinese evaluation results.

partially conflicting between machine and human evaluations, these results mean that RBMT with SPE has an equivalent performance of SMT system.

In fact, improvements for target word selection, out of vocabulary words and structural transfer are realized by SPE that complemented lack of rules in the target domain, as shown in Table 6. Meanwhile, mistranslations caused by statistical features also occurred in SPE output.

5 Issues for Context-aware Machine Translation

Our translation system has the following context-aware features, which have been used in our commercial systems (Yoshimura et al., 2011).

- Target word selection based on domain estimation
- Part-of-speech disambiguation and the reuse of translations by using preceding context

Because our system is a rule-based system, semantic dependencies between source words are used as key clues for choosing appropriate target words. Context-aware functions are used when such clue is not available. First is a function to choose a target word based on a domain of the source sentences. Some of the words in translation dictionaries are assigned domain labels, and the translation system tries to decide a domain of input sentence in morphological analysis. For example, in the case of English-Japanese translation, an English word "court" is given a Japanese translation "コート" by default, but it is translated as "法廷" if the current domain is estimated as a legal domain.

Second is used to choose a word of an appropriate part-of-speech, and to output consistent translations for proper nouns. When the translation system finds a proper noun which consists of more than one word, it memorizes a pair of source and target word, each of which is a constituent of the original proper noun. For example, if "John Snow" is in a translation dictionary and translated as "ジョン・スノー", a memorized word "Snow" will be preferably analyzed as a proper noun, and be translated as "スノー" in later context. If a sequence of words is recognized as a proper noun by named entity recognition, its constituent is treated in the same manner.

We couldn't confirm the effectiveness of the above functions in the translations of the test set due to time constraints. To get better translations, we' d like to utilize the context to make syntactic and semantic analysis more accurate.

6 Conclusion

The overview of Toshiba rule-based machine translation system with statistical post editing for scientific paper translation task is described in this paper.

A combination of RBMT and SPE achieved improvements of BLUE score in both Japanese-English and Japanese-Chinese translation. In contrast, in a part of the human evaluation, RBMT showed better performance than SPE for Japanese-English translation.

References

Hirokazu Suzuki and Akira Kumano. 2005. Learning Translations from Monolingual Corpora. In *Proceedings of MT Summit X.*

Hirokazu Suzuki. 2011. Automatic Post-Editing based on SMT and its selective application by Sentence-Level Automatic Quality Evaluation. In *Proceedings of MT Summit XIII.*

Akira Kumano. 2013. Korean Translation System for Patent Documents. In *Japio YEAR BOOK*, pages 298-301. (In Japanese)

Toshiaki Nakazawa, Hideya Mino, Isao Goto, Sadao Kurohashi and Eiichiro Sumita. 2014. Overview of the 1st Workshop on Asian Translation. IN *Proceedings of the 1st Workshop on Asian Translation (WAT2014).*

Tatsuya Izuha, Akira Kumano and Yuka Kuroda. 2008. Toshiba Rule-Based Translation System at NTCIR-7 PAT MT. In *Proceedings of NTCIR-7 Workshop Meeting*, pages 430-434.

Michel Simard, Cyril Goutte and Pierre Isabell. 2007. Statistical Phrase-based Post-editing. In *Proceedings of NAACL HLT 2007, ACL*, pages 508-515.

Michel Simard, Nicola Ueffing, Pierre Isabelle and Roland Kuhn. 2007. Rule-based Translation With

Statistical Phrasebased Post-editing. In *Proceedings of the second Workshop on Statistical Machine Translation, ACL*, pages 203-206.

Philipp Kohen, Franz Josef Och and Daniel Marcu. 2003. Statistical Phrase-Based Translation. In *Proceedings of NAACL HLT*, pages 127-133.

Philipp Kohen, Marcell Federuci, Brooke Cowan, Richard Zens, Chris Dyer, Ondrej Bojar Alexandra Constantin and Evan Herbst. 2007. Moses: Open Source Toolkit for Statistical Machine Translation. In *Proceedings of the ACL*, pages 177-180.

Graham Neubig, Yosuke Nakata and Shinsuke Mori. 2011. Pointwise Prediction for Robust, Adaptable Japanese Morphological Analysis. In *Proceedings of ACL-HLT.*

Yumiko Yoshimura, Satoshi Kinoshita and Miwako Shimazu. 1997. Processing of Proper Nouns and Use of Estimated Subject Area for Web Page Translation. In *Proceedings of TMI-97: The Seventh International Conference on Theoretical and Methodological Issues in Machine Translation*, pages 240-251.

SRC	そこで，流体の性質や条件の違いにより適切なセンサを選択することが必要である。
REF	Then, it is necessary to choose the appropriate sensor in accordance with a difference in the property and condition of the fluid.
RBMT	Then, it is required to choose a suitable sensor by the character of a fluid or the difference among conditions.
+SPE	Then, it is necessary to choose the appropriate sensor by the properties of the fluid and the difference between the conditions.

(a) Improvement of target word selection.

SRC	りん酸基をもつ界面鋳型樹脂によるＣｕ（ＩＩ）の吸着量はｐＨの増大に伴い増大した。
REF	The amount of Cu(II) adsorption by the interface template resin with phosphate group increases with an increase in pH value.
RBMT	The amount of adsorption of Cu(II) by interface mold resin with a phosphoric acid group increased with increase of pH.
+SPE	The adsorption amount of Cu (II) by the mold resin with phosphoric acid group increased with increasing pH.

(b) Mistranslation of noun phrase.

SRC	標題光スイッチングと光記録画像を形成し，その安定性を調べた。
REF	The optical switching of the title and its optical recording image were formed, and the stability was examined.
RBMT	Title optical switching and an optical record picture were formed, and the stability was investigated.
+SPE	Titled optical switching and the optical recording images were formed, and the stability is investigated.

(c) Mistranslation of tense agreement.

Table 5: A comparison between RBMT and RBMT with SPE in Japanese-English translation.

SRC	またＸＭＬの処理の時間も無視できず，実装上の工夫が必要であろう．
REF	此外，不能忽ＸＭＬ的理，在安装上也需要下功夫。
RBMT	外不能也无ＸＭＬ的理的，要需要上的法。
+SPE	外，也不能忽了ＸＭＬ的理，需要安装上下功夫。

(a) Improvement of target word selection.

SRC	ポリエーテルスルホン（ＰＥＳ）非対称ＵＦ膜は高い水浸透率と強度を持つ。
REF	聚（ＰＥＳ）非称ＵＦ膜具有高的水浸透率和度。
RBMT	聚suluhon(PES)不称UF膜有高的水渗透率和度。
+SPE	聚（ＰＥＳ）不称ＵＦ膜具有高的水的渗透率和度。

(b) Improvement of out of vocabulary words.

SRC	図１（ａ）にＪＣＰのチャネル構成を示す．
REF	１（ａ）所示ＪＣＰ的道。
RBMT	在１（ａ）表示ＪＣＰ的成。
+SPE	１（ａ）所示，ＪＣＰ的道成。

(c) Improvement of structural transfer.

SRC	最低メタンロスはメタン産生量の２％へ低下した。
REF	最低甲浪降低到了甲生量的２％以下。
RBMT	最低甲失甲生成量的２％下降了。
+SPE	最低甲失甲生量的２％。

(d) Mistranslation of verb-phrase.

Table 6: A comparison between RBMT and RBMT with SPE in Japanese-Chinese translation.

Weblio Pre-reordering Statistical Machine Translation System

Zhongyuan Zhu
Weblio Inc.
chugen.shu@weblio.co.jp

Abstract

This paper describes details of the Weblio Pre-reordering Statistical Machine Translation (SMT) System, participated in the English-Japanese translation task of 1st Workshop on Asian Translation (WAT2014). In this system, we applied the pre-reordering method described in (Zhu et al., 2014), and extended the model to obtain N-best pre-reordering results. We also utilized N-best parse trees simultaneously to explore the potential improvement for pre-reordering system with forest input.

1 Introduction

In this paper, we describe the details of Weblio Pre-reordering Statistical Machine Translation (SMT) System, experiments and some issues we faced. For this SMT system, we applied the pre-reordering method proposed in (Zhu et al., 2014). In particular, this method automatically learns pre-reordering model from word alignments and parse trees. Statistical language model is integrated in the pre-reordering model in order to reorder each node layer in parse trees. In the 1st Workshop on Asian Translation (WAT2014) (Nakazawa et al., 2014), we mainly applied this method in English-Japanese translation subtask. The parse tree we used is head-restructured CFG parse tree for English, which is also proposed in (Zhu et al., 2014). After the pre-reordering phase, we trained a conventional Phrase-based model to do the final translation.

To make some improvements, we enabled the pre-reordering system to output N-best reordering results. Also, we feed the whole translation pipe line with N-best parse trees generated by Egret parser. As a result, multiple translation hypotheses can be collected for one input sentence. Finally, we select the best hypothesis according to a balanced score.

In our experiments, the system utilizes N-best pre-reordering results shows the ability to obtain more accurate translation result. After incorporating N-best parse trees, improvements on the automatic evaluation scores are also observed.

In section 2 and 3, we briefly describe the method used for tree parsing and pre-reordering. In the remaining sections, we give some details of the experiments of our system.

2 Head-restructured CFG parse tree

In order to reorder SVO (subject-verb-object) order into SOV (subject-object-verb) order, correctly reordering long-distance words those play important roles in a sentence is crucial. Thus, the reordering model is required to capture the reordering patterns for those words. Obviously, using dependency tree should be a quick solution for this problem. As in a dependency tree, all closely related words of a specific head word come underneath that head word. All we need to do is to find the best order for the branches under those related words. In particular, if the head word is the root of the whole sentence (usually a verb), then it's reasonable to think each dependent word leads to a branch that contains a important part of the whole sentence.

However, using dependency tree naively does not work well in practice. First of all, not all components in a sentence need to be reorder. In the case of English-Japanese translation, noun phrases are usually in the identical order of English. Secondly, some local grammar structures tend to keep their unique order. For example, the combination of an adjective word with a noun usually has the same order in Japanese. But a noun follows the preposition "of" in English will appear before it in the order of Japanese. A model merely based on dependency parse trees will be sparse and hard

Proceedings of the 1st Workshop on Asian Translation (WAT2014), pages 33–38,
Tokyo, Japan, 4th October 2014.

to deal with unknown words correctly. POS (part-of-speech) tags and also structural information are still necessary.

The approach in (Zhu et al., 2014) addresses this problem by injecting sentence-level dependencies into CFG parse trees. Local grammatical structures are still kept unchanged in the parse tree. This new parse tree is called "Head-restructured CFG parse tree" in the original paper. In this paper, we use "HRCFG tree" in short to represent it. An example of HRCFG tree is shown in Figure 1.

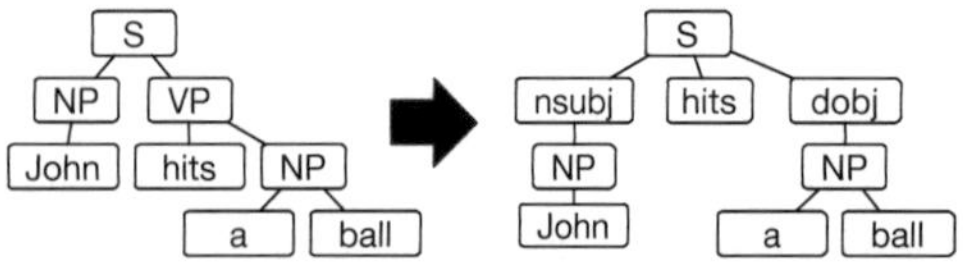

Figure 1: An example of HRCFG tree converted from CFG parse tree (A direct parent nodes of terminal nodes are now include)

In Figure 1, A normal CFG parse tree is shown in the left, and the corresponding HRCFG tree in the right. In this example, tree components explicitly shows subject, object and verb parts in the sentence. This structure with explicit annotations makes the reordering model easier to capture long-distance reordering patterns.

3 Reordering model integrated with language model

The reordering model we used in our MT systems follows the same fashion of the model in (Zhu et al., 2014). A language model is integrated to identify the best order of a node layer according to the order of target language. Although the using of language model still involves spare problem and fails to give the correct probability in some cases, it makes the implementation fairly simple.

With a bilingual training data and automatically learned word alignments given by GIZA++ (Och and Ney, 2004), we find the best order for each node layer in all parse trees, make them fit the order of aligned parts in the target sentence. Specifically, for tree nodes $\mathbf{n} = (n_1, n_2, ..., n_k)$, terminal nodes beneath n_i is defined as $\mathbf{t}^i$. Let $\mathbf{w}^i$ represent a set of words in target side which are aligned with any terminal node in $\mathbf{t}^i$. I this step, for each node layer $\mathbf{n}$, we redetermine the order of $\mathbf{n}$ according to the average position of aligned words $\mathbf{w}^i$ for each node n_i.

Then we exports a sequence of reordered non-terminal tags. For some kinds of node, non-terminal tags in the sequences are replaced by head word. After we trained a language model on them, the language model can be used to estimate the likelihood that a tag sequence follows the order of target language.

We show an example of this reordering process in Figure 2.

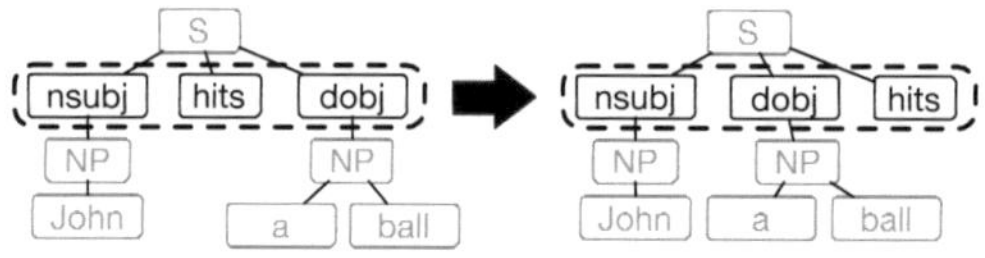

Figure 2: An example of HRCFG tree reordering

To reorder the node layer underneath the "S" node in Figure 2, we list all possible orders for the tag sequence "nsubj hits dobj" (6 possibilities in all). Then we use the language model we trained on reordered tag sequences to estimate the probability for each possible order. Finally, it is expected that the sequence "nsubj dobj hits" gets the highest language model score, as it is most closer to the order in Japanese.

The reordering operation in this fashion is applied to all node layers in the HRCFG tree. We export all terminal words in the reordered parse trees as new training data in the source side. Like Head-finalization (Isozaki et al., 2010), we also incorporate seed words in the results. So the final reordering result of the sentence shown in Figure 1 will be "John va_nsubjpass a ball va_dobj hits".

3.1 N-best reordering

In the reordering model we described above, the best order for the whole sentence is actually comprised by all *1*-best orders of every node layers in the parse tree. Although the language model usually works perfectly to give the best reordering result. In some cases, the best reordering result is unclear until the translation phase.

We give an example here, for the sentence "The rocket is launched by NASA", two plausible reordering results are shown in Table 1.

The first reordering result in Table 1 is preferred by the reordering model as "nsubjpass auxpass launched prep_by" is usually reordered into "nsubjpass prep_by launched auxpass". Unfortunately,

Table 1: Two reordering results of the sentence "The rocket is launched by NASA"

#	reordering result and corresponding translation
1	The rocket va_nsubjpass NASA by launched is ロケットは NASA によって発射された
2	NASA by The rocket va_nsubjpass launched is NASA はロケットを発射した

in this case, the translation follows the second reordering result is more natural in Japanese.

For the cases like what we show in Table 1, it's hard to find out a best order before translation. Considering N-best reordering results is necessary in order to obtain the best translation result. In our MT system, we implement this feature simply by collecting N-best reordering results for all node layers, and finally rank the reordering results by accumulated language model score.

4 Experiments

4.1 Experimental settings

For our baseline system, we use *1*-best parse trees for training and test. Stanford tokenizer and Berkeley parser (Petrov et al., 2006) are selected in the pre-processing phase in order to produce CFG parse trees. Then we obtain dependency parse trees by applying Stanford rules (Klein and Manning, 2002) to CFG parse trees. HRCFG trees are built upon these two kinds of parse trees. For the Japanese text, we use Kytea (Neubig, Nakata, and Mori, 2011) to tokenize it.

Due to the limitation of computational resource, we are only able to train our reordering model on 1.5M bilingual text (with relatively high scores in ASPEC parallel corpus) for English-to-Japanese translation task. We used this trained reordering model to reorder all training data in the source side.

We use conventional Phrase-based model implemented in Moses toolkit to finish remaining SMT pipe line. Distortion limit is set to 6 in all our experiments.

For system translates forest inputs, we use Egret parser to generate N-best packed forests. We unpack each forest and parse each individual tree to HRCFG tree. For all candidate of parse trees, we reorder them and merge same reordering results. Then for all reordering results we obtained, we translate them and record translation scores given by Moses. Finally, a best translation result is selected out by the sum of translation score and reordering score.

4.2 Experiment results

We carried out several experiments combining the use of N-best parse trees and N-best reordering results. A list of automatic evaluation scores for different system settings are listed in Table 2.

Table 2: Experiment results for different system settings

#	System	BLEU(%)	RIBES
1	*1*-best parse + *1*-best reorder	34.46	0.7817
2	N-best parse + *1*-best reorder	34.80	0.7851
3	*1*-best parse + N-best reorder	34.90	0.7857
4	N-best parse + N-best reorder	**35.10**	**0.7887**

In particular, for systems marked with "N-best parse", 30 parse trees with highest parsing scores are used. For systems marked with "N-best reorder", 10 reordering results with highest reordering scores are accepted for each parse tree. That is, for System 4, a maximum of 300 reordering results are generated for one sentence.

In WAT2014, we submitted System 3 and System 4 to human evaluation. Note that in Table 2, our in-house automatic evaluation scores are slightly different from that on the score board of WAT2014 due to different automatic evaluation pipe line we used. Official evaluation scores are listed in Table 3. Where "BASELINE" refers to Phrase-based SMT system (Koehn, Och, and Marcu, 2003) as the official baseline for human evaluation.

Table 3: Official evaluation scores in WAT2014 (kytea used for post-processing)

# System	BLEU(%)	RIBES	HUMAN
3	34.87	0.7869	**+43.250**
4	**35.04**	**0.7900**	+36.000
BASELINE	**29.80**	**0.6919**	+0.000

Our experiment results shown in Table 2 show that incorporating N-best parse tree and reordering results gained improvements for both BLEU and RIBES metrics.

In the official human evaluation, although System 4 achieved better results in automatic evaluations. Human evaluation score of it degraded compared to System 3, which only considers *1*-best parse tree.

In Figure 3 and 4, we show the growth of BLEU and RIBES when increasing candidate number considered for N-best parse trees and reordering results. Both BLEU and RIBES scores are tending to converge after we increased the N-best parse tree candidates to 30 for System 2. For System 3, the automatic evaluation scores are still increasing after 10 reordering results are considered.

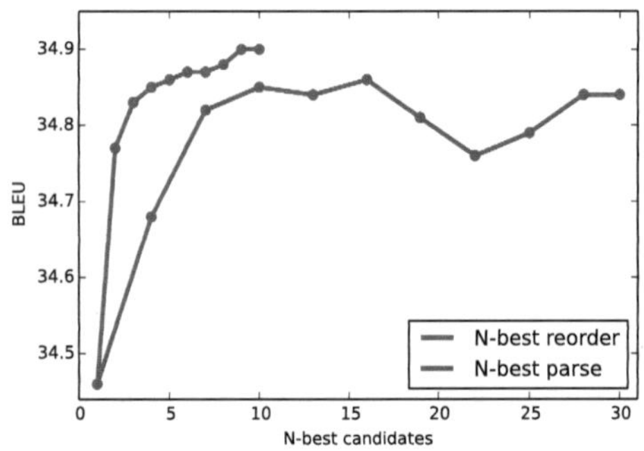

Figure 3: Growth of BLEU with increasing N-best candidates

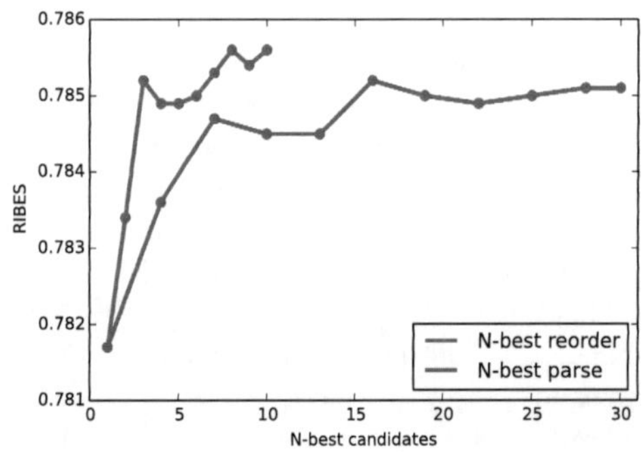

Figure 4: Growth of RIBES with increasing N-best candidates

4.3 Evaluation for pre-reordering

In this section, we evaluate the performance of pre-reordering. Follows the method described in (Isozaki et al., 2010), we estimate Kendall's τ from word alignments. A comparison of Kendall's τ distribution upon first 1.5M sentences of ASPEC corpus is shown in Figure 5.

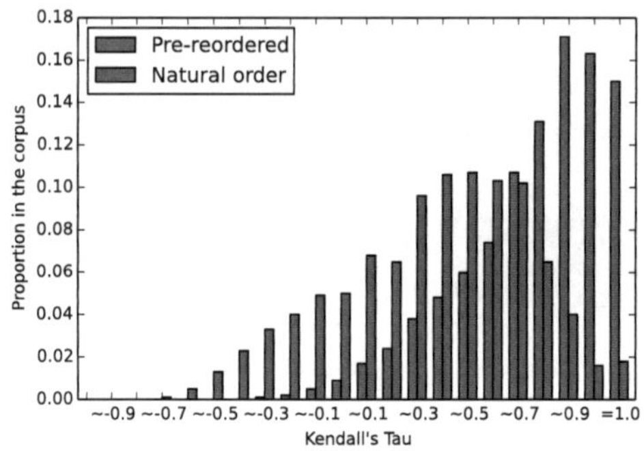

Figure 5: A comparison of Kendall's τ distribution

Average Kendall's τ of natural order and adjusted order is 0.30 and 0.71 respectively. Note that in (Isozaki et al., 2010), the algorithm for estimating Kendall's τ does not take the words with multiple alignments into account. Hence, the graph of Kendall's τ only gives a rough idea of the performance of pre-reordering. In particular, the algorithm skipped 20.30% aligned words for corpus in natural order and 14.06% aligned words for pre-reordered corpus. However, the distribution of Kendall's τ in Figure 5 gives a intuitive picture of the improvements of word order. Sentences which are fully identical in word order increased from 1.8% to 15% after pre-reordering (labeled with "=1.0" in Figure 5).

5 Error analysis

5.1 Issues of pre-reordering

Although our pre-reordering SMT system is able to produce relatively better translation results compared to baseline SMT systems. In many cases, the translation results still suffer from the defect of the reordering model. As the reordering model described in Section 3 is actually a language model built on sequences mixed with non-terminal tags and words. Involving words in the model makes the reordering more flexible, but also makes the model sparse. For some rare or unknown words, the reordering model usually fails to reorder sentences correctly.

In Table 4, we show 2 reordering samples. In Sample 1, the sentence is correctly reordered. The word "were" in English side should be placed in the end of the reordered sentence, which is expected to be translated to "された" in Japanese. In Sample 2, we replace the verb "confirmed" in Sample 1 to "observed", then the reordering model

Table 4: Samples of reordering result

#	Samples of reordering result
1	**the changes were confirmed** → the changes va_nsubjpass confirmed were
2	**the changes were observed** → the changes va_nsubjpass were observed

fails to place the word "were" into the rightmost position.

The errors like what we show in Table 4 are actually widespread in the reordering results for the ASPEC test corpus. Although in the decoding phase, the lexical distortion model of Phrase-based SMT model can partially mitigate some local errors, some critical errors still can be observed from the final translations.

5.2 Issues for Context-aware Machine Translation

In this section, we describe some efforts for utilizing context information during the translation.

We made an attempt to tackle the phrase selection problem for English-Japanese translation. In Japanese, many English words have multiple translations. Especially Japanese words in the form of Katakana usually also have corresponding expressions comprised of Chinese characters. For instance, the phrase "remote control" can be translated to both "ENKAKUSEIGYO"(遠隔制御) and "RIMOKON"(リモコン). We show the distribution of these two translations across different domains in Figure 6.

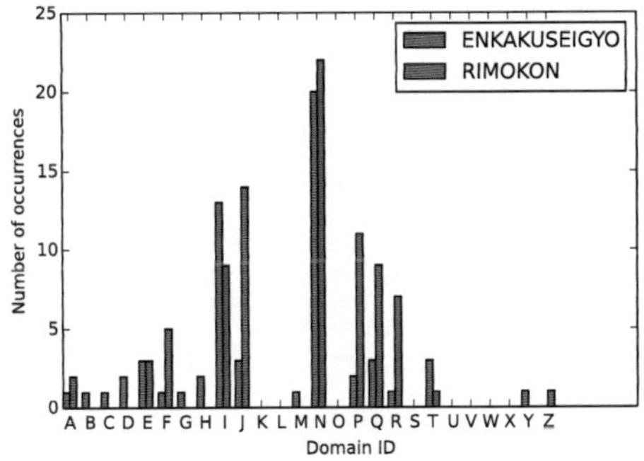

Figure 6: Translation distribution for "remote control" across several categories

From Figure 6, it's reasonable to think the phrase "RIMOKON" is more preferred in domain J, P, Q and R. While in domain N, the two phrases appear almost same times.

A simple solution is to make language model more domain-specific. We carried out experiments that simply interpolate general language model and in-domain language model. The experiment results for first three domains are shown in Figure 7.

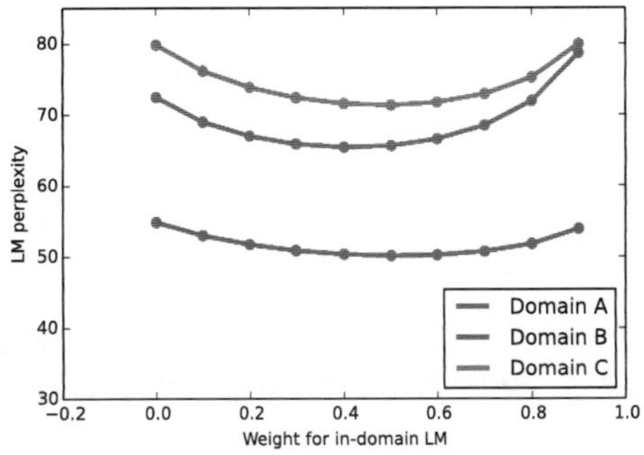

Figure 7: LM perplexity on domain-specific test data using interpolated language models

In Figure 7, we show the language model perplexity achieved on domain-specific test data using different settings. Different interpolation weights for the in-domain language model are tried. We can see the interpolated language model generally achieves best perplexities when the weight for in-domain language model is set to 0.5. Applying these interpolated language models for translation tasks in corresponding domains should help improving the quality of translation.

6 Conclusion

In this paper, we described the reordering model we applied in Weblio Pre-reordering SMT system, and also some efforts to utilize N-best parse trees and N-best reordering results. According to our in-house experiment results, the automatic evaluation scores are generally improved when multiple candidates of parse tree and reordering result are considered. However, in the human evaluation, incorporating N-best parse trees did not gain improvements.

As we demonstrated in Section 5.1, the reordering model is still unstable, and fails to work correctly even for some simple cases. Further improvement is required to enable the reordering model to deal with general cases correctly. Then, in Section 5.2, we show interpolating general and in-domain language models can be a quick solution to improve translation quality when domain information is given as context.

For future research, we still plan to explore the performance limit of pre-reordering models. With a complex reordering model considers multiple factors of the language, it's still plausible for this approach to grow in performance. Also, as the pre-reordering model used in this paper is independent of specific language pair, more experiments can be conducted on different language pairs.

References

Isozaki, Hideki et al. (2010). "Head finalization: A simple reordering rule for sov languages". In: *Proceedings of the Joint Fifth Workshop on Statistical Machine Translation and Metrics-MATR*. Association for Computational Linguistics, pp. 244–251.

Klein, Dan and Christopher D Manning (2002). "Fast exact inference with a factored model for natural language parsing". In: *Advances in neural information processing systems*, pp. 3–10.

Koehn, Philipp, Franz Josef Och, and Daniel Marcu (2003). "Statistical phrase-based translation". In: *Proceedings of the 2003 Conference of the North American Chapter of the Association for Computational Linguistics on Human Language Technology-Volume 1*. Association for Computational Linguistics, pp. 48–54.

Nakazawa, Toshiaki et al. (2014). "Overview of the 1st Workshop on Asian Translation". In: *Proceedings of the 1st Workshop on Asian Translation (WAT2014)*.

Neubig, Graham, Yosuke Nakata, and Shinsuke Mori (2011). "Pointwise prediction for robust, adaptable Japanese morphological analysis". In: *Proceedings of the 49th Annual Meeting of the Association for Computational Linguistics: Human Language Technologies: short papers-Volume 2*. Association for Computational Linguistics, pp. 529–533.

Och, Franz Josef and Hermann Ney (2004). "The alignment template approach to statistical machine translation". In: *Computational linguistics* 30.4, pp. 417–449.

Petrov, Slav et al. (2006). "Learning Accurate, Compact, and Interpretable Tree Annotation". In: *Proceedings of the 21st International Conference on Computational Linguistics and the 44th Annual Meeting of the Association for Computational Linguistics*. ACL-44. Sydney, Australia: Association for Computational Linguistics, pp. 433–440.

Zhu, Zhongyuan et al. (2014). "A preordering method using head-restructured CFG parse tree for SMT". In: *Proceedings of the 20th Annual Meeting of the Association for Natural Language Processing*, pp. 594–597.

System Description: Dependency-based Pre-ordering for Japanese-Chinese Machine Translation

Jingsheng Cai Yujie Zhang Hua Shan Jinan Xu
School of Computer and Information Technology, Beijing Jiaotong University
{12120397, yjzhang, 13120422, jaxu}@bjtu.edu.cn

Abstract

This paper describes the Beijing Jiaotong University Japanese-Chinese machine translation system which participated in the 1st Workshop on Asian Translation (WAT 2014). We propose a pre-ordering approach based on dependency parsing for Japanese-Chinese statistical machine translation (SMT). Our system achieves a BLEU of 24.12 and a RIBES of 79.48 on the Japanese-Chinese translation task in the official evaluation.

1 Introduction

Difference in word order between source language and target language will cause troubles in word alignment and further affect the quality of statistical machine translation (SMT). Therefore, it becomes an issue in SMT, especially in the language pairs where there are great difference in word order between source language and target language.

Syntax-based pre-ordering has demonstrated effectiveness in previous research. These kinds of approaches first parse the sentences in the side of source language. Then pre-ordering rules are applied to the created parse trees, in order to obtain source language sentences which have similar word order with target language sentences. Finally, the reordered source language sentences are used in the SMT system, not only in training, but also in tuning and translating. In other words, all of the sentences in the training set, the development set and the test set should be reordered while applying these kinds of approaches.

Since parsing is required in pre-ordering approaches, two popular parsing are often considered, i.e. constituent parsing and dependency parsing. Constituent parsing has been employed in pre-ordering for the translation of English-French (Xia and McCord, 2004), Germany-English (Collins et al., 2005), Chinese-English (Wang et al., 2007), etc. and shown its effectiveness. In recent years, more and more pre-ordering research used dependency parsing for the translation of Arabic-English (Habash, 2007), English-SOV languages (Xu et al., 2009) and Chinese-English (Cai et al., 2014), because the accuracy of dependency parsing is greatly improved.

This paper introduces a Japanese-Chinese SMT system which employs a pre-ordering approach based on dependency parsing. Since Japanese is a language with a fairly free word order, dependency parsing can describe the relation between two Japanese cases in a sentence better than constituent parsing. Therefore, we adopt dependency parsing for pre-ordering. Experimental results show that our approach can improve the BLEU score on the test set by 0.18, compared with the baseline system (without pre-ordering).

Section 2 describes some issues in Japanese-Chinese translation and proposes our dependency-based pre-ordering approach. Section 3 reports on our experiment results on a Japanese-Chinese phrase-based SMT (PBSMT) system. Section 4 concludes this paper.

2 Dependency-based Pre-ordering Approach

Japanese is a kind of SOV language and Chinese is a kind of SVO language. Therefore, great difference exists in their word order. Moreover, both of them have very free word order, i.e. a sentence may have several expressions by only changing its word order. This fact causes troubles while translating Japanese into Chinese.

This section describes some issues in the translation of Japanese-Chinese and then proposes our dependency-based pre-ordering approach to tackle these problems.

Proceedings of the 1st Workshop on Asian Translation (WAT2014), pages 39–43,
Tokyo, Japan, 4th October 2014.

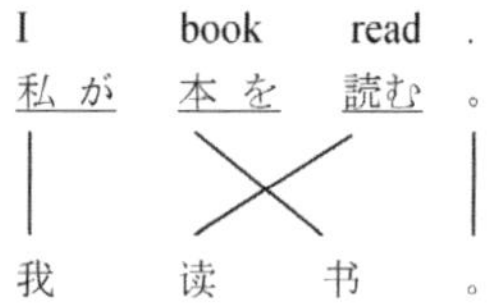

Figure 1: An example Japanese sentence and its Chinese counterpart, along with their word alignment.

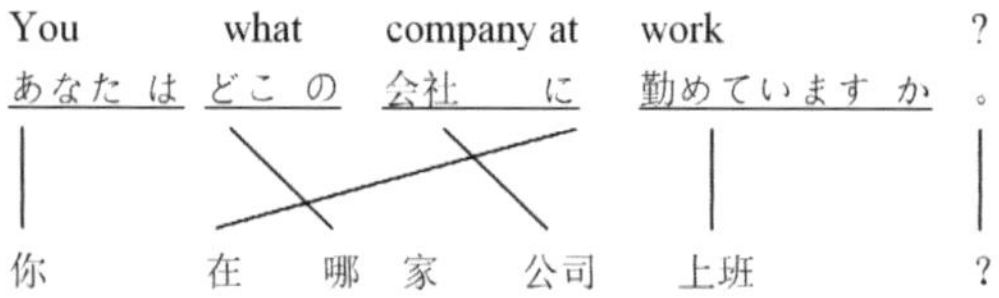

Figure 2: An example with a cross word alignment, owing to the existence of a Japanese particle "に".

2.1 Issues in Japanese-Chinese Translation

As is known to all, Japanese is a kind of SOV language, in which the verb (V) occurs after the object (O), and Chinese is a kind of SVO language, in which the verb (V) occurs before the object (O). This is the most common difference between Japanese and Chinese. Figure 1 shows an example of a Japanese sentence and its corresponding Chinese sentence with their word alignment. These sentences means "I read book.". As described in above, the verb "read" occurs after the object "book" in Japanese but before the object in Chinese. This kind of phenomena is often observed in Japanese-Chinese parallel corpus, which unavoidably brings about wrong results word alignment and further affect the quality of machine translation.

Japanese is a kind of agglutinative language but Chinese is not. A Japanese sentence consists of phrases which are usually ended with a particle, indicating the case of the phrase. Although all Japanese particles are not content words, the particles are often incorrectly aligned with Chinese content words in conventional word alignment. To relieve this problem, we consider alignment to connect the particles with Chinese prepositions. Figure 2 shows such an example, of which the Japanese sentence consisting of four phrases - "wa" case, "no" case, "ni" case and "bunmatu" case. It means "What company do you work for?" in English. The tokens within one phrase are displayed by one underline. The Japanese particle

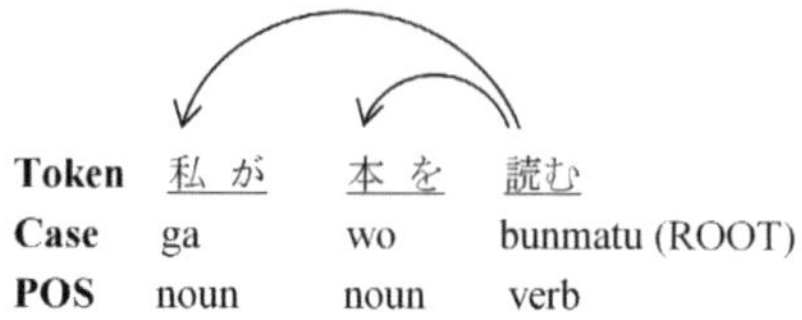

Figure 3: Dependency parse tree for the Japanese sentence in Figure 1.

"に" is aligned to the Chinese preposition "在", which is a cross word alignment within the "ni" case ("どこの会社に"). Erroneous word alignments often appear in such kinds of sentences.

2.2 Dependency-based Pre-ordering

After investigating the issues in Japanese-Chinese translation, we attempt to tackle them by introducing a pre-ordering approach into the PBSMT system. Considering that current Japanese dependency parsing is of high accuracy and provides case information, we think these conditions are suitable for both global and local pre-ordering operations. We therefore propose a dependency-based pre-ordering approach.

Figure 3 shows the dependency parse tree of the Japanese sentence in Figure 1. There are three cases in this sentence. Both of the "ga" case and the "wo" case depend on the last phrase called as "bunmatu" case, i.e. the ROOT. According to the dependency tree, we can easily move the "wo" case after the "bunmatu" to obtain an SVO word order sentence. After operating this pre-ordering, the Japanese sentence can be translated into "我/I 读/read 书/book 。/." in Chinese, whose word order is the same as its Chinese counterpart.

We investigate the phenomena of word order exchanging, such as "wo" case and "ni" case, on the ASPEC Japanese-Chinese paper excerpt corpus[1]. We take statistics of the various cases and observe the samples of the cases with high frequency. Based on the observed results, we build pre-ordering rules, which consist of global pre-ordering and local pre-ordering.

Inspired by the work of Xu et al. (2009), we obtain the global pre-ordering rules in the following way. We focus on verbs and classify the cases that directly depend on verbs into several groups. We then set sequence numbers to the groups by considering the word orders of their Chinese translations in a Chinese sentence, as we observe from

[1]http://lotus.kuee.kyoto-u.ac.jp/ASPEC/

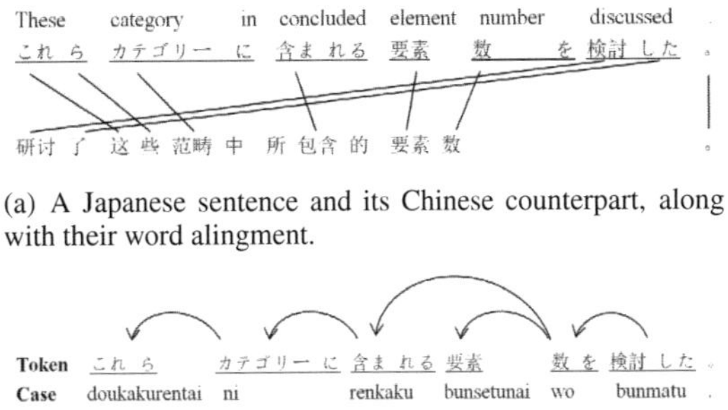

(a) A Japanese sentence and its Chinese counterpart, along with their word alingment.

(b) Dependency parse tree for the Japanese sentence.

Figure 4: An example of pre-ordering operation on a Japanese sentence.

the corpus. Table 1 lists the groups and their sequence numbers.

We first define the subtree of a case as the phrase ended with the particle and those phrases that directly or indirectly depend on this phrase. Then we design pre-ordering operation. For a given Japanese dependency tree, if its root node contains a verb, conduct pre-ordering as the following steps.

Step 1. Global Pre-ordering: Change the order of the subtrees of the cases directly depend on the "bunmatu" case and the "bunmatu" case itself, according to the sequence number of the groups that they belong to, as listed in Table 1. The cases of Group 1 should occur before those of Group 2, and so forth. Note that if any two cases belong to the same group, we keep their relative order unchanged.

Step 2. Local Pre-ordering: For "wo" case, "de" case, "ni" case, "he" case, "kara" case and "made" case, move the particles to the front of the whole subtree.

Figure 4 gives an example of conducting pre-ordering operation. Figure 4 (a) displays the Japanese sentence to be reordered, the corresponding Chinese translation and the word alignment between them. The English meaning is "(We) discussed the number of the elements that are contained in these categories.". The dependency tree of the Japanese sentence is shown in Figure 4 (b). First, global pre-ordering is conducted. The subtree of the "wo" case, i.e. all of the tokens occurring before "を", is moved to the position after the "bunmatu" case. Then, local pre-ordering is conducted. The particle "を" and "に" are moved to the front of the subtree of their cases, respectively. The reordered Japanese sentence can be translated

Group	Case
1	ga/が wa/は
2	renyou/conjunction
3	de/で ni/に he/へ kara/から made/まで yori/より to/と
4	bunmatu/文末
5	wo/を

Table 1: Groups of the cases and their sequence numbers.

into "研讨了/discussed 这些/these 范畴/category 包含/conclude 要素/element 数/number 。/." in Chinese, whose word order is more similar to its Chinese counterpart.

3 Experiments

Section 2 describes our dependency-based pre-ordering approach for the translation of Japanese-Chinese. This section reports on our experiments and evaluation results.

We use MOSES PBSMT system (Koehn et al., 2007) in our experiments and use BLEU scores (Papineni et al., 2002) and RIBES score (Isozaki et al., 2010) for evaluation.

The data sets are from the ASPEC Japanese-Chinese paper excerpt corpus. The training data contains 672,315 sentences, the development data contains 2,090 sentences and the test data contains 2,107 sentences.

We use a bilingual-based approach proposed in Su et al. (2013) for Chinese word segmentation, in which n-gram feature from the raw Chinese part and word alignment from the parallel corpus are introduced to augment the conventional model based on annotation data.

We employ the KNP parser[2] for Japanese dependency parsing. The KNP parser can create dependency tree for a Japanese sentence and provide the part-of-speech (POS) for each word, both of which are used in our dependency-based pre-ordering approach.

After Japanese dependency trees are obtained, we conduct pre-ordering on the training set, the development set and the test set by applying the pre-ordering rules described in Section 2.2. The reordered data sets are then used in training, tuning and test in the Japanese-Chinese PBSMT system.

On the other hand, data sets without pre-

[2]http://nlp.ist.i.kyoto-u.ac.jp/EN/index.php?KNP

System	BLEU on Dev	BLEU on Tst	RIBES on Tst
Baseline	21.55	20.71	77.34
Pre-ordering	21.71	20.89	77.67

Table 2: Comparisons of the pre-ordering system and the baseline system.

Category	Positive	Unchanged	Negative
Global	115	49	36
Local	63	108	29

Table 3: Human evaluation for 200 reordered sentences, respectively.

ordering are used in our baseline system for comparison.

Table 2 presents the evaluation results of the pre-ordering system and the baseline system, including the BLEU scores on the development set, the BLEU scores and the RIBES scores on the test set. The results show that the system employing our dependency-based pre-ordering approach outperforms the baseline system slightly, both on the development set and the test set. Note that these results are different with those in the official evaluation because we should keep the consistency in Chinese word segmentation, while the official evaluation uses other word segmenters (kytea and Stanford).

To access the accuracy of our pre-ordering approach, we also conduct human evaluation for the reordered sentences. 200 global reordered sentences and 200 local reordered sentences are extracted from the training data, along with their corresponding Chinese sentences. For global pre-ordering, we align the Japanese cases with the Chinese phrases. For local pre-ordering, we pick the reordered Japanese cases and align the words in them with the Chinese words. For both categories of pre-ordering, we count the number of cross alignment and compare it with the one of the original sentence pairs. Table 3 shows the results of our human evaluation. Here, "Positive" means that the number of the sentences in which the cross alignment decreases after applying the pre-ordering, "Negative" means that the number of the sentences in which the cross alignment increases after applying the pre-ordering, and "Unchanged" means that the number of the sentences in which the cross alignment stays the same after applying the pre-ordering. As shown in Table 3, global pre-ordering helps improve the word alignment in 57.5% sentences and 24.5% stays the same. Local pre-ordering helps improve the word alignment in 31.5% sentences and 54% stays the same. The results access the accuracy and effectiveness of our approach. Note that the "Unchanged" local pre-ordering is 108, which is over half of all. The reason for this is that in fact many Japanese particles have no alignment relation with any Chinese word, pre-ordering of these particles will not change the number of cross alignment at all.

4 Conclusion

This paper describes the Beijing Jiaotong University Japanese-Chinese PBSMT system participated in WAT 2014. The system employs a dependency-based pre-ordering approach. The approach conducts two categories of pre-ordering: 1) global pre-ordering reorders the cases directly depending on the verb of "bunmatu" case; 2) local pre-ordering moves the Japanese particles to the front of the case they belong to. Experimental results show that our pre-ordering approach improves the BLEU score by 0.18 and the RIBES score by 0.34 on the test set of the ASPEC Japanese-Chinese corpus. The accuracy and effectiveness of this approach are also accessed by human evaluation.

Note also that some cases which are not listed in Table 1 may also be parsed to depend on a verb of "bunmatu" case. We do not operate any preordering in such situation currently because their frequency is very low and it is difficult to summarize their reordering phenomena.

Our research builds up a framework for Japanese-Chinese pre-ordering. However, the improvement for the PBSMT system is not as great as our expectation. As shown in Table 3, some negative results are brought into the word alignment after pre-ordering. This implies that the there are some problems in current pre-ordering rules. More features from dependency tree may be introduced as constrains to the pre-ordering approach in the future.

Acknowledgments

This work is supported by Key Lab of Intelligent Information Processing of Chinese Academy of Sciences (CAS), Institute of Computing Technology, CAS, Beijing 100190, China and International Science & Technology Cooperation Program of China (Grant No. 2014DFA11350).

References

Jingsheng Cai, Masao Utiyama, Eiichiro, Sumita, and Yujie Zhang. 2014. Dependency-based Preordering for Chinese-English Machine Translation. In *Proceedings of the 52nd Annual Meeting of the Association for Computational Linguistics*, pages 155-160.

Michael Collins, Philipp Koehn, and Ivona Kucerova. 2005. Clause restructuring for statistical machine translation. In *Proceedings of the 43rd Annual Meeting of the Association for Computational Linguistics*, pages 531-540.

Nizar Habash. 2007. Syntactic preprocessing for statistical machine translation. In *Proceedings of the 11th Machine Translation Summit (MT-Summit)*.

Hideki Isozaki, Tsutomu Hirao, Kevin Duh, Katsuhito Sudoh, and Hajime Tsukada. 2010. Automatic evaluation of translation quality for distant language pairs. In *Proceedings of the 2010 Conference on Empirical Methods in Natural Language Processing*, pages 944-952.

Philipp Koehn, Hieu Hoang, Alexandra Birch, Chris Callison-Burch, Marcello Federico, Nicola Bertoldi, Brooke Cowan, Wade Shen, Christine Moran, Richard Zens, Chris Dyer, Ondrej Bojar, Alexandra Constantin, and Evan Herbst. 2007. Moses: Open source toolkit for statistical machine translation. In *Proceedings of the 45th Annual Meeting of the Association for Computational Linguistics Companion Volume Proceedings of the Demo and Poster Sessions*, pages 177-180.

Kishore Papineni, Salim Roukos, Todd Ward, and Wei-Jing Zhu. 2002. BLEU: a method for automatic evaluation of machine translation. In *Proceedings of 40th Annual Meeting of the Association for Computational Linguistics*, pages 311-318.

Chen Su, Yujie Zhang, Zhen Guo and Jinan Xu. 2013. *Exploring Multiple Chinese Word Segmentation Results Based on Linear Model.* Natural Language Processing and Chinese Computing, 400:5059.

Chao Wang, Michael Collins, and Philipp Koehn. 2007. Chinese syntactic reordering for statistical machine translation. In *Proceedings of the 2007 Joint Conference on Empirical Methods in Natural Language Processing and Computational Natural Language Learning*, pages 737-745.

Fei Xia and Michael McCord. 2004. Improving a statistical MT system with automatically learned rewrite patterns. In *Proceedings of Coling 2004*, pages 508-514.

Peng Xu, Jaeho Kang, Michael Ringgaard, and Franz J. Och. 2009. Using a dependency parser to improve SMT for subject-object-verb languages. In *Proceedings of HLT-NAACL*, pages 245-253.

Predicate-Argument Structure-based Preordering for Japanese-English Statistical Machine Translation of Scientific Papers

Kenichi Ohwada, Ryosuke Miyazaki and **Mamoru Komachi**
{ohwada-kenichi, miyazaki-ryosuke}@ed.tmu.ac.jp, komachi@tmu.ac.jp
Graduate School of System Design
Tokyo Metropolitan University, Japan

Abstract

Translating Japanese to English is difficult because they belong to different language families. Naïve phrase-based statistical machine translation (SMT) often fails to address syntactic difference between Japanese and English. Preordering methods are one of the simple but effective approaches that can model reordering in a long distance, which is crucial in translating Japanese and English. Thus, we apply a predicate-argument structure-based preordering method to the Japanese-English statistical machine translation task of scientific papers. Our method is based on the method described in (Hoshino et al., 2013), and extends their rules to handle abbreviation and passivization frequently found in scientific papers. Experimental results show that our proposed method improves performance of both (Hoshino et al., 2013)'s system and our phrase-based SMT baseline without preordering.

1 Introduction

Preordering method is one of the popular techniques in statistical machine translation. Preordering the word order of source language in advance can enhance alignments on a pair of languages with a large difference in syntax like japanese and English, and thus improve performance of machine translation system.

One of the advantages of preordering is that it can incorporate rich linguistic information on the source side, whilst off-the-shelf SMT toolkit can be plugged in without any modification. Preordering methods employ various kinds of linguistic information to achieve better alignment between source and target languages. Specifically, previous work in the literature uses morphological analysis (Katz-Brown and Collins, 2008), dependency structure (Katz-Brown and Collins, 2008) and predicate-argument structure (Komachi et al., 2006; Hoshino et al., 2013) for preordering in Japanese-English statistical machine translation.

However, these preordering methods are tested on limited domains: travel (Komachi et al., 2006) and patent (Katz-Brown and Collins, 2008; Hoshino et al., 2013) corpora. Translating Japanese to English in a different domain such as scientific papers is still a big challenge for preordering-based approach. For example, academic writing in English traditionally relies on passive voice to give an objective impression, but one can use either passive construction or a zero-pronoun in the Japanese translation of passive construction on the English side. It is not clear whether existing preordering rules are applicable to scientific domain due to such stylistic difference.

Predicate-argument structure-based preordering is one of the promising approaches that can solve syntactic and stylistic difference between a language pair. Predicate-argument structure analysis identifies who does what to whom and generalizes grammatical relations such as active and passive construction. Following (Hoshino et al., 2013), we perform predicate-argument structure analysis on the Japanese side to preorder Japanese sentences to form an SVO-like word order. We propose three modifications to the preordering rules to extend their model to better handle translation of scientific papers.

The main contribution of this work is as follows:

- We propose an extension to (Hoshino et al., 2013) in order to deal with abbreviation and passivization frequently found in scientific papers.

Proceedings of the 1st Workshop on Asian Translation (WAT2014), pages 44–49,
Tokyo, Japan, 4th October 2014.

2 Previous work

There are several related work that take preordering approaches to Japanese-English statistical machine translation.

First, Komachi et al. (2006) suggested a preordering approach for Japanese-English speech translation in travel domain based on predicate-argument structure. They used an in-house predicate-argument structure analyzer and reordered Japanese sentences using heuristic rules. They only performed preordering at sentence-level, whereas other Japanese-English preordering methods we will describe below perform preordering at both sentence- and phrase-level[1].

Second, Katz-Brown and Collins (2008) presented two preordering methods for Japanese-English patent translation based on morphological analysis and dependency structure, respectively. Morphological analysis-based method splits sentences into segments by punctuation and a topic marker ("は"), and then reverses the segments. Dependency analysis-based method reorders segments into a head-initial sentence, and moves verbs to make an SVO-like structure. Unlike (Komachi et al., 2006), they also reverse all words in each phrase.

Third, Hoshino et al. (2013) proposed predicate-argument structure-based preordering rules in two-level for the Japanese-English patent translation task. The first is sentence-level and the second is phrase-level. Furthermore, sentence-level preordering rules are divided into three parts. In total, sentences are reordered sequentially by four rules. Since this method is the one we re-implemented in this paper, we will describe their method in detail below.

Pseudo head-initialization Since Japanese is a head-final language but English is a head-initial language, this rule transforms a Japanese dependency tree as to become a head-initial phrase sequence. Concretely, we move the last phrase, which is a predicate of a Japanese sentence in almost all cases, to the beginning of the sentence. We then order each phrase as their children located immediately after them.

Inter-chunk preordering We move a predicate of a sentence to an adequate place. If a subject exists in a sentence[2], the predicate is moved immediately after the subject. If a subject is not present but an object, the predicate is moved just before the object. If there is neither a subject nor an object, the predicate is moved just before the rightmost phrase in the predicate's children. Thanks to this rule, even when a subject and a object do not exist, we avoid having a predicate at the beginning of a sentence.

Inter-chunk normalization We restore the order of coordinate expressions which are reversed by the first rule. Also, since a full stop is moved along with the predicate, we restore it back to the end of the sentence.

Intra-chunk preordering We apply the phrase-level rule, which swaps function words and content words in a phrase. It will improve alignments because function words in Japanese (e.g. postposition) appear after content words while those in English (e.g. preposition) appear before content words.

3 Extension to (Hoshino et al., 2013)

Our proposed preordering model is based on (Hoshino et al., 2013) with three extensions to better handle academic writing in scientific papers.

3.1 Parenthesis preordering

Scientific papers often include parenthetical expressions. The training data (1,000,000 parallel sentences, hereafter referred to as 1M training corpus) contains 168,336 (16.8%) parentheses on Japanese side, and 187,400 parentheses on English side. However, Japanese dependency analyzer fails to parse parenthetical expressions appropriately. In particular, if a parenthesis is used to show apposition (e.g. abbreviation and acronym), the pseudo head-initialization described in the last section swaps an acronym and its full spelling, which is not desirable. Therefore, we modify the pseudo head-initialization rule to restore the position of parenthetical expressions.

Figures 1a and 1b illustrate how parenthesis preordering transforms original sentences. Parenthesis preordering rule handles not only single phrase parenthetical expressions but also multiple phrase parenthetical expressions.

3.2 Passive voice preordering

In scientific papers, zero-pronouns in Japanese are often translated into passive construction in English. The number of passive construction in the

[1] In this paper, "phrase" means "bunsetsu".

[2] A pro-drop language like Japanese often omits subjects.

Figure 1: Examples of extended preordering rules.

(a) Parenthesis preordering (single phrase)

Japanese: 一般病棟における | コンサルテーション型の | 緩和ケアチーム | （ＰＣＴ）が | 注目されている。
English literal: in the general ward | of the consultation type | palliative care team | (PCT)$_{NOM}$ | notice$_{PRESENT|PASSIVE}$.
English translation: "Palliative care team (PCT) of the consultation type in the general ward is noticed."

Pseudo head-initialization: 注目されている。 | （ＰＣＴ）が | 緩和ケアチーム | コンサルテーション型の | 一般病棟における
Parenthesis preordering: 注目されている。 | 緩和ケアチーム | （ＰＣＴ）が | コンサルテーション型の | 一般病棟における

(b) Parenthesis preordering (multiple phrases)

Japanese: ＰＡＬチャートを | 使った | 適切な | ガラス部材（庇を | 含めた）を | 選択する | 手法を | 紹介した。
English literal: PAL chart$_{ACC}$ | using | appropriate | glass member (a hood$_{ACC}$ | including)$_{ACC}$ | selecting | method$_{ACC}$ | present$_{PAST}$.
English translation: "This paper presents a technique for selecting an appropriate glass member (including a hood) using a PAL chart."

Pseudo head-initialization: 紹介した。 | 手法を | 選択する | 含めた）を | ガラス部材（庇を | 使った | ＰＡＬチャートを | 適切な
Parenthesis preordering: 紹介した。 | 手法を | 選択する | ガラス部材（庇を | 含めた）を | 使った | ＰＡＬチャートを | 適切な

(c) Passive voice preordering

Japanese: 研究班の | 概要を | 紹介した。
English literal: research team$_{GEN}$ | outline$_{ACC}$ | introduce$_{PAST}$
English translation: "The outline of the research team is introduced."

Pseudo head-initialization: 紹介した。 | 概要を | 研究班の
Passive voice preordering: 概要を | 研究班の | 紹介した。

(d) Subject preordering

Japanese: ＣＯＰＤ患者の | 換気増加は | 日常活動を | 制限する | 重要な | 因子である。
English literal: COPD patient$_{GEN}$ | ventilation increase$_{TOP}$ | daily activity$_{ACC}$ | limit$_{PRES}$ | important | be$_{PRES}$ factor.
English translation: "Ventilation increase of the COPD patients is the important factor which limits the daily activity."

Pseudo head-initialization: 因子である。 | 換気増加は | ＣＯＰＤ患者の | 制限する | 日常活動を | 重要な
Inter-chunk preordering: 換気増加は | 因子である。 | ＣＯＰＤ患者の | 制限する | 日常活動を | 重要な
Modified inter-chunk preordering: 換気増加は | ＣＯＰＤ患者の | 因子である。 | 制限する | 日常活動を | 重要な

Final preordering result: は換気増加 | のＣＯＰＤ患者 | ある因子で | 制限する | を日常活動 | な重要。

1M training corpus is 166,057 (17%), whereas the number of active construction starting with "They ..." and "It is ..." are 4,700 and 17,104 (2%), respectively. Hence, we move a predicate to the end of the sentence if there exists no subject in active voice.

Figure 1c describes how this rule transforms a Japanese sentence with a zero-pronoun. Even though the Japanese side is in active voice, English translation is expressed in passive voice. Note that a Japanese sentence in active voice may be translated into different expressions even in the same passive construction (e.g. "... を説明した (explained ...)" can be either "... was explained" or "It was explained that ...".).

3.3 Subject preordering

Hoshino et al. (2013) proposed to move a predicate after the subject (*inter-chunk preordering*). However, if a subject is modified by other phrases, this rule moves the predicate to the middle of a subjective phrase composed of multiple phrases. Thus, we move a predicate to the end of the subjective phrase.

Table 1d depicts how subject preordering moves a predicate in a sentence. As we can see, this rule prevents subjective phrase "ＣＯＰＤ患者の | 換気増加 (Ventilation increase of the COPD patients)" to be split by the predicate movement.

4 Experiments

We compared translation performance using a standard phrase-based statistical machine translation technique with three kinds of data:

- original data (baseline),
- preordered data by our re-implementation of (Hoshino et al., 2013), and
- preordered data by our proposed methods.

We analyzed predicate-argument structure of only the last predicate for each sentence, regardless of the number of predicates in a sentence. Also, following (Hoshino et al., 2013), we did not consider event nouns as predicates.

4.1 Experimental settings

We used 1M Japanese-English parallel sentences extracted from scientific papers (`train-1.txt`) from the Asian Scientific Paper Excerpt Corpus (ASPEC) [3]. We varied the size of the training corpus and used the best size determined by preliminary experiments.

We identified predicate-argument structure in Japanese by SynCha[4] 0.3. It uses MeCab[5] 0.996 with IPADic 2.7.0 for morphological analysis and CaboCha[6] 0.68 for dependency parsing.

We used SRILM[7] 1.7.0 for language model, GIZA++[8] 1.0.7 for word alignment, and Moses[9] 2.1.1 for decoding. We set distortion limits to default value 6 for all systems[10].

Translation quality is evaluated in terms of BLEU (Papineni et al., 2002) and RIBES (Isozaki et al., 2010), as determined by the workshop organizers (Nakazawa et al., 2014).

We performed minimum error rate training (Och, 2003) optimized for BLEU using the development set (`dev.txt`) of the ASPEC corpus. We conducted all the experiments using the scripts distributed at KFTT Moses Baseline v1.4 [11].

4.2 Experimental results

Table 1 shows the experimental results. In terms of BLEU, our re-implementation of (Hoshino et al., 2013) is below the baseline method while our proposed methods better than the baseline. In terms of RIBES, all preordering methods outperform the baseline, and our proposed method archieve the highest score.

All methods including parenthesis preordering outperform the baseline method, and when we subtract three modifications one by one from proposed method, the parenthesis rule has the largest impact on the translation quality.

4.3 Discussion

Some of the errors found in a translation result are due to the errors in predicate-argument structure analysis. We found that it is hard for predicate-argument structure analyzer trained on a newswire

[3] `http://lotus.kuee.kyoto-u.ac.jp/ASPEC/`
[4] `http://www.cl.cs.titech.ac.jp/~ryu-i/syncha/`
[5] `http://mecab.googlecode.com/`
[6] `http://cabocha.googlecode.com/`
[7] `http://www.speech.sri.com/projects/srilm/`
[8] `https://code.google.com/p/giza-pp/`
[9] `http://www.statmt.org/moses/`
[10] We confirm in another experiment that the highest performance of the proposed system is archieved by the distortion limit around 15.
[11] `http://www.phontron.com/kftt/`

Table 1: Comparison of the preordering methods. All the preordering models using (Hoshino et al., 2013) are our re-implementation of their paper.

Method	**BLEU**	**RIBES**
Phrase-based SMT baseline (w/o preordering)	15.74	0.620162
(Hoshino et al., 2013) (preordering baseline)	15.45	0.645954
Proposed method – parenthesis preordering	15.73	0.652461
Proposed method – passive voice preordering	15.93	0.654454
Proposed method – subject preordering	15.88	0.650964
Proposed method	16.02	0.654600
Phrase-based SMT baseline (ORGANIZER)	18.45	0.645137

Figure 2: Error analysis of predicate-argument structure-based preordering.

(a) Reordering error with "It is . . ." construction.

Japanese: ＬＡＮの | 仕組みに関する | 解説記事である。
English literal: LAN$_{GEN}$ | on mechanism | be$_{PRES}$ explanation article.

Final reordering result: に関する仕組み | のＬＡＮ | ある解説記事で。
English translation: It is the explanation article on the mechanism of the LAN.

(b) Reordering error with "They . . ." construction.

Japanese: 新しい | 規格の | 項目と | 構成を | 示した。
English literal: new | standard$_{GEN}$ | item and | composition$_{ACC}$ | show$_{PAST}$.

Final reordering result: と項目 | を構成 | の規格 | 新しい | た示し。
English translation: They showed item and composition of the new standard.

corpus to parse scientific papers. It may be necessary to perform domain adaptation at some level.

Apart from apparent errors in predicate-argument structure analysis, there exist errors in preordering rules. Figure 2 shows errors in preordering. In both examples, the passive voice preordering rule moves the predicate to the end of a sentence, but the English counterpart uses active construction instead of passive construction. It would be necessary to not only perform predicate-argument structure analysis on the source side but also on the target side to correctly align predicate-argument structures between a language pair.

5 Issues for Context-aware MT

In this paper, we did not consider any inter-sentential context, even though the off-the-shelf predicate-argument structure analyzer is able to perform co-reference and zero-anaphora resolution (Iida and Poesio, 2011). It is only because the training corpus at hand does not come with inter-sentential information. If we have access to the whole article, we may perform zero-anaphora resolution to better handle passivization in Japanese-English translation.

6 Conclusion

In this paper, we propose to modify several rules to (Hoshino et al., 2013) in order to address the stylistic differences for translating scientific papers. Experimental results show that all preordering methods combined improve the system performance.

In future work, we investigate the effectiveness of these rules in different domains.

References

Sho Hoshino, Yusuke Miyao, Katsuhito Sudoh, and Masaaki Nagata. 2013. Two-Stage Pre-ordering for Japanese-to-English Statistical Machine Translation. In *Proceedings of The 6th International Joint*

Conference on Natural Language Processing (IJC-NLP2013), pages 1062–1066.

Ryu Iida and Massimo Poesio. 2011. A Cross-Lingual ILP Solution to Zero Anaphora Resolution. In *Proceedings of the 49th Annual Meeting of the Association for Computational Linguistics: Human Language Technologies (ACL-HLT 2011)*, pages 804–813.

Hideki Isozaki, Tsutomu Hirao, Kevin Duh, Katsuhito Sudoh, and Hajime Tsukada. 2010. Automatic Evaluation of Translation Quality for Distant Language Pairs. In *Proceedings of the Conference on Empirical Methods in Natural Language Processing (EMNLP)*, pages 944–952.

Jason Katz-Brown and Michael Collins. 2008. Syntactic Reordering in Preprocessing for Japanese→English Translation: MIT System Description for NTCIR-7 Patent Translation Task. In *Proceedings of the NTCIR-7 Workshop Meeting*, pages 409–414.

Mamoru Komachi, Masaaki Nagata, and Yuji Matsumoto. 2006. Phrase Reordering for Statistical Machine Translation Based on Predicate-Argument Structure. In *Proceedings of the International Workshop on Spoken Language Translation*, pages 77–82.

Toshiaki Nakazawa, Hideya Mino, Isao Goto, Sadao Kurohashi, and Eiichiro Sumita. 2014. Overview of the 1st workshop on asian translation. In *Proceedings of the 1st Workshop on Asian Translation (WAT2014)*.

Franz Josef Och. 2003. Minimum Error Rate Training in Statistical Machine Translation. In *Proceedings of the 41st Annual Meeting on Association for Computational Linguistics*, pages 160–167.

Kishore Papineni, Salim Roukos, Todd Ward, and Wei-Jing Zhu. 2002. BLEU: a Method for Automatic Evaluation of Machine Translation. In *Proceedings of the Annual Meeting of the ACL*, pages 311–318.

A machine translation system combining rule-based machine translation and statistical post-editing

Terumasa EHARA
Yamanashi Eiwa College
999, Yokone, Kofu, Yamanashi, JAPAN

eharate @ yamanashi-eiwa.ac.jp

Abstract

System architecture, experimental settings and evaluation results of the EIWA in the WAT2014 Japanese to English (ja-en) and Chinese to Japanese (zh-ja) tasks are described. Our system is combining rule-based machine translation (RBMT) and statistical post-editing (SPE). Evaluation results for ja-en task show 19.86 BLEU score, 0.7067 RIBES score, and 22.50 human evaluation score. Evaluation results for zh-ja task show 33.57 BLEU score, 0.8114 RIBES score, and 15.00 human evaluation score.

1 Introduction

One of the architectures of combining rule-based technique and statistical technique in the machine translation field is combining a rule-based machine translation (RBMT) and a statistical post-editing (SPE) (Dugast et al., 2007; Simard et al., 2007; Ehara, 2007).

The RBMT part translates source documents to target documents using rule-based machine translation. The SPE part automatically post-edits the output of the RBMT part to be more accurate target documents.

2 System architecture and experimental setting for the ja-en task

Our basic system architecture for ja-en task is shown in Figure 1 that is the same in the previous works (Ehara, 2007; Ehara, 2010; Ehara, 2011; Ehara, 2013). We use commercial based translation software for the RBMT part and the phrase based Moses (Koehn et al., 2003) for the SPE part. The distortion limit in the tuning process and decoding process for the SPE part is set to 1, because both the source and target languages on the SPE part are the same.

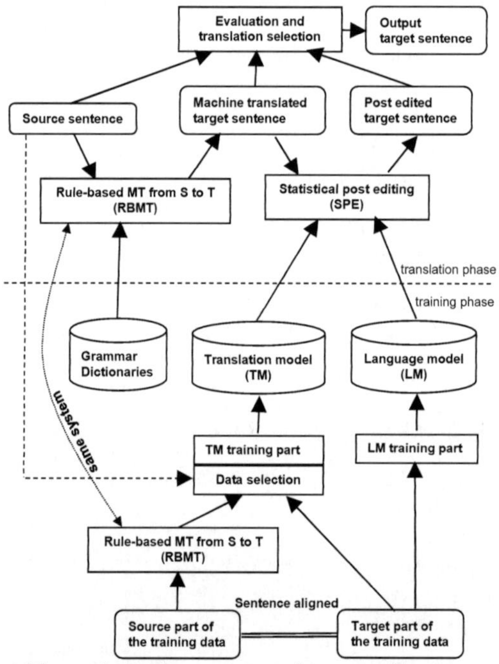

Figure 1: Basic system architecture for the ja-en task

2.1 Translation model adaptation

Translation model (TM) training for SPE part does not use whole training data for ja-en task (3,008,500 sentence pairs) but selected data adapted to the development data or the test data. For the SPE for the development data, 134,634 sentence pairs are used and for the SPE for the test data, 127,925 sentence pairs are used. The method of this filtering differ from the previous method (Ehara, 2010). The new method is as follows: At

Proceedings of the 1st Workshop on Asian Translation (WAT2014), pages 50–54,
Tokyo, Japan, 4th October 2014.

a first step, we select training sentences which include a low frequency word in the development sentences (or the test sentences). The low frequency word means the count of such word in the training sentences are less than a threshold (we set 300). The word "ＳＡＲＳ", which occurs 13 times in the development set, occurs 189 times in the training set. So, it is a low frequency word in the development data. On the other hand, the word "化学", which occurs 29 times in the development set, occurs 40,964 times in the training set. So, it is not a low frequency word in the development data. At a second step, we add training sentences which include a word in the development sentences that is not in the set made by the first step. However, we do not add any sentences by the second step. For example, the word "標題" occurs 19 times in the development set and is not included in the set made by the first step but it occurs no times in the whole training set. We make a TM from this adapted training data. We refer to this TM as TM1. The training sentence pairs for the TM1 for the test data are selected by the similar method.

We make another TM. Adding to the training sentences of TM1, we add additional training sentences from the RBMT outputs of the development data (or the test data). This means SPE part makes easier not to rewrite RBMT outputs. We refer to this TM as TM2. The training data for the TM2 of the development set includes 134,634 sentence pairs and the training data for the TM2 of the test set includes 129,737 sentence pairs.

2.2 Language model

For language model (LM) training for SPE part uses 2,000,000 sentences from train-1.txt and train-2.txt. We use SRILM (Stolcke, 2002) with 5-grams order and modified Kneser-Ney discounting.

2.3 Translation selection

We use a translation selection method with a quality estimation method described in Ehara (2013). Translation candidates are from three translations: RBMT output and two SPE outputs. One SPE method uses TM1 and the other SPE method uses TM2, which are described in 2.1. The bonus score (Ehara, 2013) for two SPE outputs are set to 0.1. As the result, 126, 850 and 836 outputs are selected from the outputs of RBMT, SPE with TM1 and SPE with TM2, respectively.

3 System architecture and experimental setting for the zh-ja task

For the zh-ja task, we use the same base system of ja-en task. But, we do not use TM adaptation by the data selection part in the Figure 1 and translation selection by the translation evaluation and selection part in the Figure 1, as the ja-en task. We, however, add some new things to our base system:

・To use a user dictionary in the RBMT part.

・To adapt a language model.

・To make additional sentence segmentation by the full-width space position.

3.1 User dictionary

A user dictionary for the RBMT part is made from the zh-ja training data. We make the phrase table from the training data using phrase-based Moses and extract high scored phrase pairs. We filter these selected phrase pairs using part of speech. As a result, we get the user dictionary having 1,246,274 entries all of which are nouns.

3.2 Translation model

We use whole 672,315 zh-ja training sentence pairs to make the TM for the SPE part. After additional sentence segmentation described the section 3.4, we get 679,292 training segment pairs. We do not use training data filtering like in the ja-en task.

3.3 Language model adaptation

For LM training, in addition to zh-ja training data, we add more sentences from the Japanese side of the ja-en training data. The method for adding is like TM adaptation for the ja-en task. For example, LM for the development set is adapted as follows. In the first step, we select training sentences of ja-en task (only Japanese side) which include a low frequency word in the RBMT output of the Chinese side of the development data. The low frequency word means the count of such word in the training sentences are less than a threshold (we set 300). In a second step, we add training sentences of ja-en task (only Japanese side) which include a word in the RBMT outputs of the Chinese side of the development data and that is not in the set made by the first step. LM adaptation for the test set is similar.

As the result, we get 1,109,647 Japanese sentences to train LM for the development set and 1,092,850 Japanese sentences to train LM for the test set. By this adaptation, mean value of the perplexity for the Japanese side of the development set drops from 66.72 to 59.69.

3.4 Additional sentence segmentation

Several sentences in the zh-ja task include a full-width space character ("　") which is used to separate segments. For example, the following sentences in the development set include such full-width space.

「北方的水生食物连锁污染数据库　调查工具」

「北方の水食物連鎖汚染データベース　調査道具」

So, we make an additional segmentation to the training, development and test sets. When the number of the full-width spaces between Japanese side and Chinese side in training or development sentence pair is the same, the sentences are segmented at the full-width space position. For the test set, we make this segmentation at all full-width space position in Chinese sentences.

4 Issues for context-aware machine translation

TM adaptation described in 2.1 and LM adaptation described in 3.3 can be considered context-aware machine translation. Our method can be extended to document level adaptation. However, we do not make experiments that use non adapted models or adapted models not with the test set level but the test document level. One shortcoming of our adaptation method is that it needs retraining of TM and/or LM adapted to the input document, which is time consuming.

5 Evaluation results

Automatic evaluation results for the whole test sentences (zh-ja: 2107, ja-en: 1812) and human evaluation results for the selected test sentences (400) by the organizer are shown in Table 1 with our system rank and the number of all evaluated systems up to September 14th.

Task	BLEU	RIBES	HUMAN
ja-en	19.86 (9/27)	0.7067 (5/27)	22.50 (7/16)
zh-ja	33.53 (12/19)	0.8114 (6/19)	15.00 (5/11)

Table 1: Evaluation results

5.1 Human evaluation results

Comparing with the baseline system, the number of wins, ties and losses in human evaluation in the zh-ja task are 197, 66 and 137, respectively. An example of EIWA's win case is shown in Table2[1]. The EIWA's result is very similar to the reference.

EIWA	この発見は角野の推測に新たな根拠を与えていると考えられる。
base line	この発見により与えられると考えられる対角野の推測のために新しい。
reference	このことは角野の推測に新たな根拠を与えるものと考えられる。
source	可以认为这个发现对角野的推测给予新的根据。

Table 2: Example of EIWA's win case

Some examples of EIWA's loss cases are shown in Table 3.

EIWA	灯油漏洩を防止処置を扱った研究は非常に多く，化学処理方法の検討中の段階であった。
base line	石油流出の防止処理対策についての研究は非常に多く，化学の防犯処理方法は研究段階にある。
reference	流出油の防除手法についてはかなり研究が進んでいるが，ケミカルの防除手法はまだ調査研究の途中段階である。
source	关于石油泄漏的防范处理措施的研究非常多，通过化学的防范处理方法正处在研究阶段。

(a) Lexical mistranslation

EIWA	着目し，地盤材料として利用する人工石炭灰粒子として，すべての粒子の特性に基づいて，粒子の形状，物理的特性と単粒子の粉砕特性について検討を行った。
base line	個々の粒子の特性に基づいて，地盤材料としての利用の人工石炭灰粒子に着目し，粒子の形状，物理特性および単個の粒子の破砕特性について検討した。
reference	造粒石炭灰を地盤材料として利用することに着目し，粒子個々の特性に基づいて，粒子の形状や物理的特性および単粒子破砕特性について検討した。
source	着眼于作为地基材料予以利用的人造煤灰颗粒，基于每个粒子的特性，对粒子的形状、物理特性以及单颗粒子的破碎特性进行了讨论。

(b) Syntactic mistranslation

Table 3: Examples of EIWA's loss cases

[1] All sample sentences (source and reference sentences) in this document are provided by the Asian Scientific Paper Excerpt Corpus.

In Table 3 (a), EIWA's translation of the Chinese expression "石油泄漏" is "灯油漏洩" compared with the baseline translation "石油流出". This case has lexical mistranslation in EIWA.

In Table 3 (b), Chinese subordinate clause including "着眼" is incorrectly parsed by EIWA's RBMT part. This case has syntactic mistranslation in EIWA.

5.2 Correlation between automatic and human evaluation results

For human evaluated 400 sentences of zh-ja task, we conduct automatic evaluations with RIBES (Isozaki et al., 2010) and IMPACT (Echizen-ya and Araki, 2007).

Here we use "human average score (HUM)" which means the average value of scores of the three human annotators. DIFF_RIBES is the difference of RIBES scores of EIWA's output and baseline output. DIFF_IMPACT, also, means the difference of IMPACT scores of EIWA's output and baseline output. All these scores are in the interval [-1,1]. The scattering graph between HUM and DIFF_RIBES is shown in the Figure 2. The scattering graph between HUM and DIFF_IMPACT is shown in the Figure 3.

Pearson's correlation coefficient between HUM and DIFF_RIBES is 0.3618 and Pearson's correlation coefficient between HUM and DIFF_IMPACT is 0.3686. They are weak correlations.

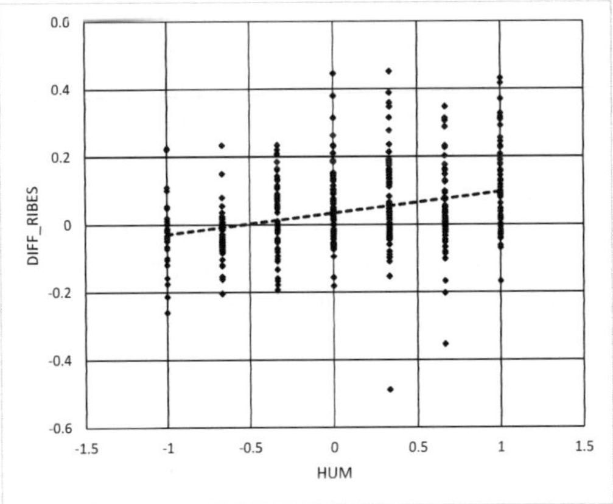

Figure 2: Correlation between HUM and DIFF_RIBES

Table 4 shows examples having big difference between HUM and DIFF_RIBES. At Table 4 (a), lexical error "暗号陽２３号" may affect HUM score to be negative, while DIFF_RIBES is positive because sentence structures of EIWA and reference is more similar than the sentence structures of baseline and reference.

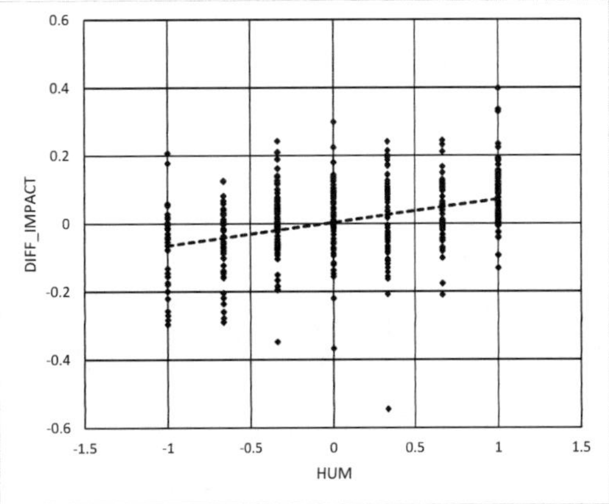

Figure 3: Correlation between HUM and DIFF_IMPACT

At Table 4 (b), the main part of the sentence, "Ｅｍｍａ／ＱｏＳを提案した" in the reference, is correctly translated in EIWA. So, HUM may be 1. It is not clear that DIFF_RIBES is negative.

At Table 4 (c), baseline translation is perfectly equal to the reference translation. So, RIBES score of baseline is 1 then DIFF_RIBES is negative. However, two annotators evaluated EIWA's win and one annotator evaluated baseline's win. The reason may be that EIWA's translation is more literal than baseline translation. Another reason may be that the references were not shown to annotators when they made evaluation. Multiple references by additional translation or scrambling of reference (Isozaki et al., 2014) may make DIFF_RIBES be smaller.

6 Conclusion

System architecture, experimental setting and evaluation results of EIWA are described. We are in the middle position in human and automatic evaluation. One of the future issues is to improve parsing accuracy in the RBMT part. Syntactically collapsed RBMT outputs cannot be recovered by the SPE part. Other future issue is to combine rule-based technique and statistical technique more tightly beyond RBMT plus SPE method.

EIWA	水稲のカドミウムの高吸収特性を示す品種「暗号陽23号」を用いた。
base line	カドミウム高吸収特性の品種「密阳23号」を示すイネを採用した.
reference	イネはカドミウム高吸収特性を示す品種「密陽23号」を用いた。
source	稻子采用了显示镉高吸收特性的品种“密阳23号”。

(a) HUM= -1, DIFF_RIBES=0.222

EIWA	本稿では, ALMプランEmma／QoSを提案し, オーバレイネットワークでは, 同時に複数のビデオを伝送を実現する場合, 分散制御のQoSである.
base line	Emma／QoSはオーバレイネットワークでは, 同時に複数のビデオを伝送を実現する方案を提案した分散制御のQoSをALM
reference	本論文では, オーバレイネットワークにおける複数ビデオの同時配信時にQoSを分散制御で実現するALMプロトコルEmma／QoSを提案した.
source	本文提出了ALM方案Emma／QoS, 在Overlay网络中, 实现同时传输复数视频时分散控制QoS。

(b) HUM=1, DIFF_RIBES= -0.1678

EIWA	表3に人工株式市場の各エージェントの予測の木で用いる記号を構成することを示した。
base line	人工株式市場を構成する各エージェントの予測の木に用いる記号を表3に示す.
reference	人工株式市場を構成する各エージェントの予測の木に用いる記号を表3に示す.
source	表3显示构成人工股份市场的各代理商的预测树中使用的记号。

(c) HUM=0.3333, DIFF_RIBES=-0.4873

Table 4: Examples having big difference between HUM and DIFF_RIBES

Reference

Loïc Dugast, Jean Senellart and Philipp Koehn. 2007. Statistical Post-Editing on SYSTRAN's Rule-Based Translation System. *Proceedings of the Second Workshop on Statistical Machine Translation*, pages 220-223.

Hiroshi Echizen-ya and Kenji Araki. 2007. Automatic Evaluation of Machine Translation based on Recursive Acquisition of an Intuitive Common Parts Continuum, *Proceedings of the Eleventh Machine Translation Summit (MT SUMMIT XI)*, pages 151-158.

Terumasa Ehara. 2007. Rule Based Machine Translation Combined with Statistical Post Editor for Japanese to English Patent Translation. *Proceedings of Machine Translation Summit XI, Workshop on Patent Translation*, pages13-18.

Terumasa Ehara. 2010. Machine translation for patent documents combining rule-based translation and statistical post-editing. *Proceedings of NTCIR-8 Workshop Meeting*, pages 384-386.

Terumasa Ehara. 2011. Machine translation system for patent documents combining rule-based translation and statistical post-editing applied to the PatentMT Task. *Proceedings of NTCIR-9 Workshop Meeting*, pages 623-628.

Terumasa Ehara. 2013. Machine translation system for patent documents combining rule-based translation and statistical post-editing applied to the NTCIR-10 PatentMT Task. *Proceedings of the 10th NTCIR Conference*, pages 335-338.

Hideki Isozaki, Katsuhito Sudoh, Hajime Tsukada and Kevin Duh. 2010. Head finalization: A simple reordering rule for SOV languages. *Proceedings of the Joint 5th Workshop on Statistical Machine Translation and MetricsMATR*, pages 244-251.

Hideki Isozaki, Natsume Kouchi and Tsutomu Hirao. 2014. Dependency-based Automatic Enumeration of Semantically Equivalent Word Orders for Evaluating Japanese Translations. *Proceedings of the Ninth Workshop on Statistical Machine Translation*, pages 287–292.

Philipp Koehn, Franz J. Och and Daniel Marcu. 2003. Statistical Phrase-Based Translation, *Proceedings of HLT-NAACL 2003*, pages 48-54.

Michel Simard, Nicola Ueffing, Pierre Isabelle and Roland Kuhn. 2007. Rule-based Translation With Statistical Phrase-based Post-editing. *Proceedings of the Second Workshop on Statistical Machine Translation*, pages 203-206.

Andreas Stolcke. 2002. SRILM - An Extensible Language Modeling Toolkit. *Proceedings of the International Conference on Spoken Language Processing.*

Japanese to English Machine Translation using Preordering and Compositional Distributed Semantics

Sho Hoshino Hubert Soyer Yusuke Miyao Akiko Aizawa
National Institute of Informatics
2-1-2 Hitotsubashi, Chiyoda, Tokyo, Japan
{hoshino,soyer,yusuke,aizawa}@nii.ac.jp

Abstract

The pipeline of modern statistical machine translation (SMT) systems consists of several stages, presenting interesting opportunities to tune it towards improved performance on distant language pairs like Japanese and English. We explore modifications to several parts of this pipeline. We include a preordering method in the preprocessing stage, a neural network based model in the tuning stage and a recurrent neural network language model in the postprocessing stage.

To our knowledge this is the first work tightly integrating a neural network based model into the tuning stage of a SMT system for the Japanese-English language pair. As a first step in this direction we provide several insights into how this integration should be approached and give rise to future work in this area.

1 Introduction

Modern models for statistical machine translation constitute a pipeline of different components. This pipeline usually involves a preprocessing part, a language model, a translation model and a postprocessing part. While this or a similar structure is basis of most systems and generally agreed upon, a lot of research has been focusing on modifying and extending the individual components.

Many parts rely on probabilities acquired through word frequencies in fixed contexts, discarding additional syntactical and semantical information. Problems arising from these strong assumptions become particularly apparent when dealing with distant language pairs like Japanese and English.

We focus exclusively on translating Japanese sentences to English and take several measures to inject additional information into the pipeline of our baseline system.

- We apply preordering to the input text as a way of compensating for syntactic differences between English and Japanese.
- We insert scores into the translation model of our baseline system that are computed from semantically meaningful distributed vector representations.
- As postprocessing, we utilize a recurrent neural network language model to re-score the 100 best translation candidates for each output sentence of our system. Being able to handle variable length context, it complements the n-gram based language model used within the pipeline.

2 System

We built our baseline system with Moses (Koehn et al., 2007) as a phrase-based machine translation system loosely following the setup described by the WAT 2014 organizers (Nakazawa et al., 2014), with some modifications.

We will quickly go through every step of our training.

1. Tokenization (section 3)
2. Training of compositional distributed vector representations (section 2.1.2)
3. Preordering (section 2.1.1)
4. Generation of 6-gram language model with SRILM
5. Training of translation model with MGIZA++
6. Tuning with compositional distributed semantics features
7. Translation of devtest and test set using Moses decoder
8. Training of RNN LM and reranking of 100 best translation candidates for every sentence

Proceedings of the 1st Workshop on Asian Translation (WAT2014), pages 55–63,
Tokyo, Japan, 4th October 2014.

9. Evaluation of final output through BLEU and RIBES scores and submission to WAT 2014 human evaluation

2.1 Extensions

In the following, we will describe the modifications to our baseline system. They are grouped into three parts, one part describing the preordering of the Japanese input text, the second part explaining the integration of a neural network based distributed compositional semantics model and lastly, the reranking of the translation candidates for each sentence using a recurrent neural network language model.

2.1.1 Preordering Japanese Text

We employ a preordering method for Japanese-to-English translation. We preorder the input text in the preprocessing stage to reduce the difference between the word order of the Japanese input sentence and the word order of the English target sentence.

Parts of a Japanese sentence can be scrambled/shuffled without changing the meaning of the sentence or making it grammatically incorrect. Therefore, one English sentence can potentially correspond to several shuffled variations of the same Japanese sentence.

Yoshida et al. (2014) show that normalizing the word order of Japanese sentences can benefit readability.

Taking scrambling into account not only increases readability, it also plays an important role in machine translation (Isozaki et al., 2014). Hayashi et al. (2013) were able to improve the results of statistical machine translation systems by generating English determiners in the Japanese input text and reordering its words. Kudo et al. (2014) applied preordering and generated zero-subjects to achieve state-of-the-art results on a web-text corpus.

We employ the preordering rules introduced in (Hoshino et al., 2014) to reduce order ambiguity in the Japanese input text. This method has achieved state-of-the-art results on the NTCIR patent corpus.

Following this method, we parse input sentences with the Japanese dependency parser KNP to obtain chunked[1] dependency and coordination labels corresponding to the dependency. After that, we apply the following three rules: Rule 1 transforms each chunked sentence into a form that is more suitable for the preordering rules that follow this step. Rule 2 reorders entire chunks while Rule 3 reorders the words inside of every chunk resulting in the final reordered version of the sentence.

Rule 1 (chunking) Given an input sentence with l chunks ($input = c_1\ c_2\ ...\ c_l$) we merge all coordinated chunks into one chunk ($c_1\ c_2\ ...\ c_l \rightarrow c_1\ c_2\ ...\ c_m$ where $m \leq l$). After that, we split punctuations[2] from chunks applying the following rules:

Rule 1-A A chunk $c_x (1 < x \leq m)$ will not be split when a predecessor chunk c_{x-1} is a noun.

Rule 1-B Even if Rule 1-A is applied to a chunk c_x, the chunk will be split into three new chunks (words,particle,punctuation) if this chunk ends with a particle[3] .

Rule 1-C A chunk c_x will always be split into words and punctuation when it ends with a punctuation.

Rule 2 (inter-chunk reordering) After Rule 1 produced a new chunked sentence, all of the n chunks between punctuations ($c_1\ c_2\ ...\ c_n$ where $c_x (1 \leq x \leq n)$ is not a punctuation) are reordered ($c_1\ c_2\ ...\ c_n \rightarrow w1\ ...\ w_{q-1}\ c_{i-1}\ ...\ c_1\ w_q\ c_n\ ...\ c_{i+1}$), where a chunk $c_i (1 \leq i \leq n)$ contains q words, ending with a particle word ($c_i = w_1, ..., w_{q-1} w_q$ where w_q is a particle).

Rule 3 (intra-chunk reordering) Given a chunk c_x which has p content words and q function words ($c_x = w_1\ ...\ w_p\ w_{p+1}\ ...\ w_{p+q}$), we swap the content words and the function words, then reverse the function words ($c_x = w_1\ ...\ w_p\ w_{p+1}\ ...\ w_{p+q} \rightarrow w_{p+q}\ ...\ w_{p+1}\ w_1\ ...\ w_p$).

Figure 1 illustrates how the introduced preordering rules are applied to an example sentence.
The sentence comprises 6 chunks two of which are labeled as coordinated by the KNP parser (表1と and 図2は).
Step 1 displays the basic, unaltered source sentence. In the second step the two coordinated

[1] This chunk actually is a bunsetsu, a linguistic unit in Japanese, as used in (Yoshida et al., 2014)

[2] We only regard Japanese comma "、" or period "。" as punctuation.

[3] We only consider the Japanese topic case marker particles "ga" and "ha".

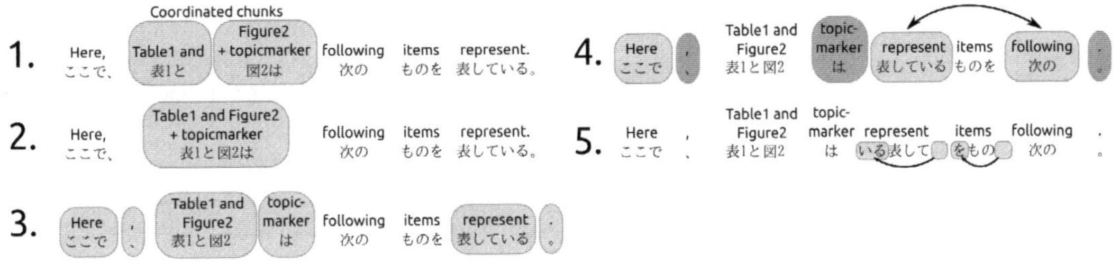

Figure 1: Illustration of the pre-ordering rules described in 2.1.1 to an example.

chunks are merged into one following Rule 1. Rule 1, Rule 1 A, B and C result in several splits (topic marker,".", ",") in step 3.
In step 4, Rule 2 causes "represent" and "following" to be switched. Finally, Rule 3 is applied in step 5 and affects only the Japanese text. いる and を, both labeled as function words by the parser.

2.1.2 Compositional Distributed Semantics

Many machine learning algorithms require fixed length vectors as input. Of the various different ways to map words to vectors, neural network based models have proven very effective recently.

Vector representations (embeddings) created by these models have been utilized as features to achieve state-of-the-art results in several different Natural Language Processing tasks (Collobert et al., 2011; Mikolov et al., 2013; Baroni et al., 2014), giving rise to many new variants. Methods have been developed that are capable of embedding words from different languages into the same vector space (Zou et al., 2013), there are models that can induce representations of whole phrases or sentences instead of only single tokens (Socher et al., 2010; Le and Mikolov, 2014; Blacoe and Lapata, 2012) and there are models implementing a mixture of these two ideas, embedding phrases from different languages into the same vector space (Hermann and Blunsom, 2014; Cho et al., 2014).

Work has been published about integrating embeddings and neural network models into the statistical machine translation pipeline for various language combinations, however, we are not aware of any previous work attempting this for the Japanese/English language pair.

As a first step in this direction, we integrate the model introduced by Hermann et al. (Hermann and Blunsom, 2014) into our baseline system, specifically, we use a slightly modified version of the "BI" model described in the paper.

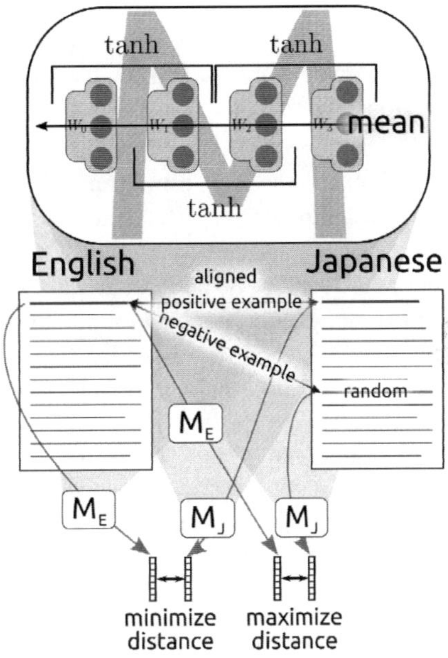

Figure 2: Illustration of model described in (Hermann and Blunsom, 2014), slightly modified to use mean instead of addition

From this point on we will refer to the model as embedding model or neural network model. Learned in an unsupervised way, we hope to indirectly inject context knowledge through the neural network model into our baseline machine translation system.

Figure 2 illustrates how the model is trained. The training is centered around a model M that looks up a word representation w_i for each word in a given sentence and combines them by wrapping a hyperbolic tangent function $(tanh)$ around the sum of the vectors of each bi-gram and computing the mean of these intermediate results. The original version described in (Hermann and Blunsom, 2014) applies addition instead of the mean. However, in preliminary experiments on an information retrieval task we obtained more promising results using the mean and therefore decided to exploit this insight.

One training step requires this model to be applied to three sentences: One English sentence, the Japanese sentence aligned to this English sentence and a Japanese sentence chosen at random from the corpus. There are two sets of word representations, a Japanese set and an English set, that are initially initialized at random by sampling values from a Gaussian centered at 0 with a standard deviation of 0.1. When looking up the vector representations to compose in the model, we choose the set of representations corresponding to the language that the currently handled sentence is in.

During training we then modify the word vectors to minimize the Euclidean distance between the vectors composed for the sentences of the valid, sentence aligned Japanese-English sentence pair and maximize the distance between the vectors of the English sentence and the randomly sampled Japanese sentence. By repeating this procedure for many sentence pairs the model learns to distinguish between valid translation pairs and invalid, randomly sampled pairs. At application time we exploit this property and compute a normalized distance between two given phrases or sub-phrases to judge their similarity.

Because this model only weakly incorporates order information on the bi-gram level it is applicable to very short phrases and even single tokens and can potentially even deal with preordered text. Due to this flexibility we can insert it into almost any part of the machine translation pipeline.

We trained the model on the 1 million parallel sentences in ASPEC that feature the highest alignment scores. We omitted the remaining 2 million sentence pairs completely to avoid introducing errors caused by incorrect alignment. Replacing tokens that occur less than 6 times in the training set resulted in more stable learning and better performance on a simple information retrieval task. After hyperparameter optimization the vectors in our embedding model were chosen to be 128 dimensional, the margin for the noise-contrastive objective was set to 1.0 and we regularized the word representations with a $l2$-regularization of 10^{-5}. For faster training we utilized RMSProp (Tieleman and Hinton, 2012) with a decay of 0.99 and a learning rate of 0.001.

We explored two ways to include the method into our baseline system.

Feature Function We created a new feature function that is utilized in the tuning phase of the log-linear translation model of our baseline. Moses allows us to access the text of each sub-phrase candidate pair evaluated during decoding. For each sub-phrase we compute its corresponding Japanese and English vector representation using our embedding model. We proceed by calculating a similarity score between the English and the Japanese sub-phrase vector. We chose the angular similarity, a normalized version ($[0, 1]$) of the cosine similarity, as it was superior to the Euclidean similarity in our previous experiments on an information retrieval task. Depending on the outcome we create one of 3 *Sparse Features*. One feature for highly similar phrases (similarity > 0.5), one for less similar phrases (similarity ≤ 0.5) and one for out-of-vocabulary cases where none of the tuples in one or both phrases could be found. This feature split is necessary to counteract problems with out-of-vocabulary cases. We encountered these cases specifically for phrases containing mostly named entities. Named entities are often not part of the pre-trained word representations. Even though moses would translate these tokens correctly (often just by transliteration) the score produced by the neural model would be not defined due to out-of-vocabulary errors. Not using this feature split lead to very poor performance.

Phrase Table We computed a score for each phrase tuple in the phrase table of our system, following (Cho et al., 2014). We iterated through all phrase combinations present in the phrase table and added an additional similarity score computed by the neural model in the same way as described above for the feature function case. This does not require extending our baseline system, the system only needs to incorporate one more feature when reading the phrase table.

2.1.3 Reranking with the Recurrent Neural Network Language Model

Neural Networks have been applied successfully in language modeling tasks over the past years (Mikolov et al., 2011a) and are increasingly often found in combination with or as an extension to statistical machine translation systems (Devlin et al., 2014; Cho et al., 2014; Zhang et al., 2014; Liu et al., 2014).

We employ the Recurrent Neural Network Language Model Toolkit (RNNLM) (Mikolov et al., 2011b) to rerank the 100 best translation candidates for each sentence and use the best candidates for our submission.

3 Data

We use only the provided ASPEC corpus and do not rely on any external resources. We train our language model with all 3 million sentences of the training set. For the translation model we only utilize the top 1 million sentences (regarding alignment scores). For hyperparameter tuning we use the development split of the corpus. Our preliminary evaluation is conducted on the *devtest* split, only the final results specified in the paper were calculated on the *test* split.

The default moses tokenization script does not perform Unicode NFKC normalization. Converting Japanese full width roman characters to half width characters is crucial to tackle transliteration cases from Japanese to English. Therefore we apply the following preprocessing steps before executing the moses tokenization script.

1. Conversion of XML entity names to Unicode characters
2. Character normalization by Unicode NFKC and deletion of double spaces
3. First letter lowercasing in all sentences without an all-uppercase first word
4. Conversion of double quotations to “ and ”
5. Commas, periods, and round brackets were regarded as tokens

In the final submissions, we applied the Moses detokenization script and converted the first letter of each sentence to upper case in order to avoid possible biases in the human evaluation.

4 Evaluation

We evaluated our results on the test split provided with the ASPEC corpus. To avoid tokenization mismatches we applied the same tokenization method to the test set that we had previously used on the training set and computed BLEU and RIBES scores with the Travatar[4] scoring script. The scores published on the WAT automatic evaluation website differ due to tokenization mismatches.

[4]http://www.phontron.com/travatar/evaluation.html

Preordering	Embeddings	BLEU	RIBES
No	None (Baseline)	19.16	63.41
No	Feature Function	18.95	63.48
No	Phrase Table (full)	18.82	63.23
Yes	Feature Function	18.92	61.76
Yes	None (Baseline)	18.55	61.44
Yes	Phrase Table (full)	-	-
No	Phrase Table (1 col)	14.53	60.59

Table 1: Scores for different ways to include the Compositional Distributed Semantics model, with and without preordering. In the *Feature Function* setting, the embedding model was integrated as a feature function into Moses; in the *Phrase Table* setting we employed the model to produce a score for each entry in the phrase table of the baseline translation model. *(full)* means that we used the default moses scores plus the newly computed score, for *(1 col)* we used only the score without the Moses default scores.

4.1 General Experiments

As listed in Table 1 our baseline achieved a score of 19.16 BLEU and 63.41 RIBES. Both of these scores can be considered low compared to results acquired e.g. on the Chinese to Japanese task of WAT 2014 where the phrase-based baseline model provided by the organizers achieved a BLEU score of 27.96. The same baseline system only achieved 18.45 on the Japanese to English task which confirms that the Japanese to English translation task is highly difficult.

Settings with preordering consistently perform worse than their counterparts without preordering, even though the employed preordering method has proven very successful (Hoshino et al., 2014) on the NTCIR patent corpus before. We suspect the main cause to be the different domain of the text. The NTCIR workshop revolved around text from the patent and legal domain while WAT 2014 is based on the ASPEC corpus comprising abstracts from scientific papers. Sentences in patent and legal text must be phrased in a very concise and unambiguous way and therefore feature a lot of recurring phrases. Writers of scientific text have more freedom to express content in English and can draw from a larger set of ways to phrase their ideas. This looser structure leads to mismatches when applying the heuristic preordering rules.

Both ways to integrate the scores computed with

the neural network model into the Moses pipeline perform roughly equally well, falling just a little short of the baseline but failing to beat it. (see *Phrase Table (full)* and *Feature Function*)

Examining phrase pairs and their scores revealed that the scores make sense in general, even identifying transliterations correctly with a high confidence. However, the model fails to capture an important property that prevents it from contributing information to Moses that is not already covered by the default features. It almost entirely neglects syntactic structure. Because of its objective to only distinguish valid translations from invalid ones, the model learns to ignore special characters, determiners and other words that do not possess a high discriminative value. The translation hypotheses of our baseline system, however, include many cases where the recognition of syntax and special characters is crucial to assign sensible scores. The values of word vectors of many stop words, determiners and special characters reveal that most of them are in close proximity to the zero vector. This vector consisting only of zeros constitutes the neutral element of the mean function as well as the hyperbolic tangent. Therefore, having or not having such a token in a sentence will only marginally change the composed representation.

This issue becomes particularly problematic for pairs of the form

Japanese	English
トークン	token
トークン	token !
トークン	the token the the

All three of these examples will have an almost identical score since the vectors of "!" and "the" were learned to be very close to the zero vector.

In an information retrieval context where processed sentences are sensible and sane, this property does not pose a huge problem. However, in the case of a phrase table or hypotheses in the tuning stage of an SMT system, cases like the one illustrated above occur regularly and should exhibit not the same but very different scores.

The *Phrase Table (1 col)* setting achieves 14.53 BLEU without utilizing the default Moses scores in the phrase table. We were surprised that having only one score value in the phrase table the system could reach a BLEU value that is not on an entirely different level than the baseline. We leave it to future research to investigate to what extend the neural model score can substitute the default Moses scores.

System	averaged Kendall's tau
Baseline	0.2990
Baseline + Preordering	0.3712

Table 2: Preordering Evaluation with Kendall's tau.

4.2 Preordering

To separate the evaluation of our preordering method from the machine translation evaluation, we calculated an intrinsic quality measure specific to preordering.

We apply the procedure previously introduced by (Isozaki et al., 2010b; Hoshino et al., 2014).

In our baseline method we rely on MGiza++ to align Japanese and English sub-phrases. Without preordering MGiza++ will perform a lot of non-monotonic alignments. The goal of preordering is to reduce the number of these non-monotonic alignments, in the best case leading to exclusively monotonic alignments. Utilizing Kendall's tau we can compare the alignments resulting from input with and without preordering. The closer this coefficient is to 1.0, the more monotonic are the alignments and the higher is the intrinsic benefit of the preordering. Table 2 lists the averaged coefficients computed with the baseline and the preordered input. It shows that our preordering performs better than the non-preordered system on this intrinsic measure.

Observations at the previously held NTCIR workshops indicated that better values in this measure correspond to better machine translation quality in terms of automatic as well as human evaluation. Our results in section 4.1 show that this intuition does not hold for the ASPEC corpus.

4.3 RNNLM Reranking

After training our baseline system including the neural network score feature function and obtaining 100 translation candidates for each input sentence of the test set, we apply the Recurrent Neural Network Language Model toolkit described in (Mikolov et al., 2011b) to re-rank these 100-best candidates according to their language model score.

Mikolov's implementation offers a variety of hyperparameters to tune the neural network training for optimal performance. Specifically, we

RIBES	BLEU	hidden	direct	Preordering
63.90	18.37	300	150	No
63.74	18.40	300	100	No
63.72	18.61	200	100	No
63.66	18.30	200	150	No
63.41	19.16	-	-	No
62.06	18.36	200	100	Yes
62.03	18.29	200	150	Yes
61.99	18.34	300	150	Yes
61.98	18.48	300	100	Yes
61.44	18.55	-	-	Yes

Table 3: Results for training the RNN LM with different hyperparameters applying it to re-rank the 100 best translation candidates for each output sentence of our SMT model. We varied the number of hidden units (*hidden*), the number of direct connections from input to output layer (*direct*) and kept the number of classes for the factored softmax fixed at 220 (following the recommendation in (Mikolov et al., 2011b) with $\#classes = \sqrt{\text{size of vocabulary}}$) and the number of steps of backpropagation-through-time fixed at 5. The *preordered* column indicates whether the preordering described in (Hoshino et al., 2014) was applied.

	BLEU	RIBES	human
Baseline	17.47	63.08	-5.750
Baseline + Preordering	17.01	61.08	-14.250

Table 4: Scores from WAT 2014 evaluation board.

adapted the number of hidden units and the number of direct connections from the input to the output layer. To choose the best settings we evaluated several configurations, the results for some of these configurations are displayed in Table 3. Reranking the translation candidates with the RNNLM improves the RIBES score while BLEU decreases instead. This pattern is consistent over all settings displayed in the table. Further, all settings with preordering perform worse than their counterparts without preordering. This goes along with previous observations presented in Table 1. The RIBES measure was specifically designed with distant language pairs like English and Japanese in mind(Isozaki et al., 2010a). With an increase of almost 0.5 from the non-preordered baseline to the best results with reranking and even more improvement for the preordered case, we conclude that reranking with an RNNLM improved our translation results significantly.

4.4 WAT 2014 Evaluation Board

The BLEU and RIBES scores on the official evaluation board as reported in Table 4 differ largely from the results presented in Table 1. This is due to tokenization mismatches.

Since our baseline system differs slightly from the system provided by the WAT 2014 organizers we submitted our baseline as a point of reference for our own experiments to the human evaluation. As our second submission to the human evaluation we chose our baseline with preordering. Preordering has proven successful in previous NTCIR workshops but has failed to improve upon the baseline in WAT 2014.

Table 4 shows that our baseline performs slightly worse than the baseline of the organizers. We are primarily interested in the difference between our baseline and our baseline with preordering. The human evaluation confirms that preordering has a negative effect when applied to the ASPEC corpus. According to the WAT 2014 homepage, the scores of the human evaluation are calculated by repeatedly comparing sentences from the submissions to their corresponding outputs of the baseline system provided by the organizers. They therefore indicate how a submission performs in comparison to the organizer's baseline. The fine grained results of the human evaluation in WAT 2014 offer a good opportunity to investigate the effects of our preordering method.

Examples illustrating the effect of the applied preordering method are shown in Table 5. We only picked examples featuring clear annotator agreement. -1 indicates that the organizers' baseline was assessed as superior to our system, 1 that it was evaluated to be inferior.

The biggest change in both of the examples shown in Table 5 was induced by the same preordering rule (Rule 2). Due to the lack of a topic marker in both source sentences Rule 2 caused the main verb to be brought to the front of the sentence.

Despite the similarity in the preprocessing step the quality of the translations differs heavily. While Example 2 was evaluated as superior to the organizers' baseline, Example 1 was received as just the opposite.

In example 1, the preordered main verb ("discussed") was omitted entirely in the output of our system, changing the meaning from a discussion to a statement.

On the contrary, the output of our system for ex-

Example 1: Negative Impact of Preordering	
human judgment	-1 -1 -1
Source	プラスチック以外の非金属製の義肢装具材料について論じた。
Preordered Source	論じた ついて に 義肢 装具 材料 の 非 金属 製 の プラスチック 以外 。
Baseline + Preordering	The non - metallic materials of a prosthesis apparatus is made of plastics.
Organizers'	The non - made of metal except for the plastic prosthesis apparatus material are discussed.
Reference	Artificial limb apparatus nonmental material other than plastic is discussed.
Example 2: Positive Impact of Preordering	
human judgment	1 1 1
Source	標記の新しいインライン流量計を開発した。
Preordered Source	開発 した を インライン 流量 計 新しい の 標記 。
Baseline + Preordering	We have developed a new in-line flowmeter.
Organizers'	The titled new in-line flowmeter was developed.
Reference	The titled new in-line flowmeter was developed.

Table 5: Positive and negative effects of preordering

ample 2 shows a very natural structure, following the word order of the preordered Japanese source almost exactly.

5 Conclusion and Future Work

In this work we investigated several modifications and insertions to the pipeline of our baseline statistical machine translation system.

In the preprocessing phase we preordered the Japanese input text to compensate for order differences in the distant Japanese-English language pair. In the tuning phase of our decoder we evaluated different ways to include phrase similarity scores computed utilizing a neural network based compositional distributed semantics model. In the postprocessing phase we reranked the translation candidates for each sentence according to scores calculated with a recurrent neural network language model.

To our knowledge this is the first attempt to utilize neural network features directly integrated into the tuning and decoding process of a SMT system in a Japanese-English translation task. We therefore regard this work a first step towards improving Japanese to English translation systems by tightly coupling them with neural networks.

Our experiments show that preordering fails to yield the same improvements in the scientific paper domain that it has previously achieved on text from the legal/patent domain. We attribute this to the difference in the rigidness of possible formulations in these domains. The heuristic rules our preordering method is based on can better capture the more rigid sentences in the patent domain while they are prone to mismatches on the less rigid sentences in the scientific paper domain.

We conclude that neural networks utilized in machine translation should take word order into account and should be trained towards objectives that do not neglect syntactic features. The semantic similarity that can be captured by the model described in (Hermann and Blunsom, 2014) appears to be already sufficiently covered by the default features of our baseline system for the case of machine translation.

Employing the recursive neural network language model introduced by Mikolov et al. (Mikolov et al., 2011a) has proven successful for reranking translation candidates and significantly improved the RIBES score in our experiments.

Recent work (Devlin et al., 2014; Cho et al., 2014; Zhang et al., 2014; Liu et al., 2014) proves, there is a lot of potential in utilizing neural network based models in the machine translation pipeline. With the lessons learned from our work we hope for successful applications of this combination to the Japanese-English language pair in the future.

References

Marco Baroni, Georgiana Dinu, and Germán Kruszewski. 2014. Don't count, predict! a systematic comparison of context-counting vs. context-predicting semantic vectors. In *Proceedings of the 52nd Annual Meeting of the Association for Computational Linguistics*.

William Blacoe and Mirella Lapata. 2012. A comparison of vector-based representations for semantic composition. In *Proceedings of the 2012 Joint Conference on Empirical Methods in Natural Language Processing and Computational Natural Language Learning*.

Kyunghyun Cho, Bart van Merrienboer, Caglar Gulcehre, Fethi Bougares, Holger Schwenk, and Yoshua Bengio. 2014. Learning phrase representations using rnn encoder-decoder for statistical machine translation. *arXiv preprint arXiv:1406.1078*.

Ronan Collobert, Jason Weston, Léon Bottou, Michael Karlen, Koray Kavukcuoglu, and Pavel Kuksa. 2011.

Natural language processing (almost) from scratch. *Journal of Machine Learning Research*, 12:2493–2537.

Jacob Devlin, Rabih Zbib, Zhongqiang Huang, Thomas Lamar, Richard Schwartz, and John Makhoul. 2014. Fast and robust neural network joint models for statistical machine translation. In *Proceedings of the 52nd Annual Meeting of the Association for Computational Linguistics*.

Katsuhiko Hayashi, Katsuhito Sudoh, Hajime Tsukada, Jun Suzuki, and Masaaki Nagata. 2013. Shift-reduce word reordering for machine translation. In *Proceedings of the 2013 Conference on Empirical Methods in Natural Language Processing*.

Karl Moritz Hermann and Phil Blunsom. 2014. Multilingual models for compositional distributed semantics. In *Proceedings of the 52nd Annual Meeting of the Association for Computational Linguistics*.

Sho Hoshino, Yusuke Miyao, Katsuhito Sudoh, and Masaaki Nagata. 2014. A preordering method robust to parsing errors for japanese-to-english statistical machine translation. In *Proceedings of the 20th Annual Meeting of the Association for Natural Language Processing*. (in Japanese).

Hideki Isozaki, Tsutomu Hirao, Kevin Duh, Katsuhito Sudoh, and Hajime Tsukada. 2010a. Automatic evaluation of translation quality for distant language pairs. In *Proceedings of the 2010 Conference on Empirical Methods in Natural Language Processing*.

Hideki Isozaki, Katsuhito Sudoh, Hajime Tsukada, and Kevin Duh. 2010b. Head finalization: A simple reordering rule for sov languages. In *Proceedings of the Joint Fifth Workshop on Statistical Machine Translation and MetricsMATR*.

Hideki Isozaki, Natsume Kouchi, and Tsutomu Hirao. 2014. Dependency-based automatic enumeration of semantically equivalent word orders for evaluating japanese translations. In *Proceedings of the Ninth Workshop on Statistical Machine Translation*.

Philipp Koehn, Hieu Hoang, Alexandra Birch, Chris Callison-Burch, Marcello Federico, Nicola Bertoldi, Brooke Cowan, Wade Shen, Christine Moran, Richard Zens, Chris Dyer, Ondrej Bojar, Alexandra Constantin, and Evan Herbst. 2007. Moses: Open source toolkit for statistical machine translation. In *Proceedings of the 45th Annual Meeting of the Association for Computational Linguistics Companion Volume Proceedings of the Demo and Poster Sessions*.

Taku Kudo, Hiroshi Ichikawa, and Hideto Kazawa. 2014. A joint inference of deep case analysis and zero subject generation for japanese-to-english statistical machine translation. In *Proceedings of the 52nd Annual Meeting of the Association for Computational Linguistics*.

Quoc V Le and Tomas Mikolov. 2014. Distributed representations of sentences and documents. *Journal of Machine Learning Research*, 32:1188–1196.

Shujie Liu, Nan Yang, Mu Li, and Ming Zhou. 2014. A recursive recurrent neural network for statistical machine translation. In *Proceedings of the 52th Annual Meeting on Association for Computational Linguistics. Association for Computational Linguistics*.

Tomas Mikolov, Anoop Deoras, Stefan Kombrink, Lukàs Burget, and Jan Cernockỳ. 2011a. Empirical evaluation and combination of advanced language modeling techniques. In *Proceedings of the 12th Annual Conference of the International Speech Communication Association*, pages 605–608.

Tomas Mikolov, Stefan Kombrink, Anoop Deoras, Lukas Burget, and Jan Cernocky. 2011b. RNNLM – recurrent neural network language modeling toolkit. In *Proceedings of IEEE Automatic Speech Recognition and Understanding Workshop 2011 Demo Session*.

Tomas Mikolov, Ilya Sutskever, Kai Chen, Greg S Corrado, and Jeff Dean. 2013. Distributed representations of words and phrases and their compositionality. In *Advances in Neural Information Processing Systems 26*, pages 3111–3119.

Toshiaki Nakazawa, Hideya Mino, Isao Goto, Sadao Kurohashi, and Eiichiro Sumita. 2014. Overview of the 1st workshop on asian translation. In *Proceedings of the 1st Workshop on Asian Translation (WAT2014)*.

Richard Socher, Christopher D Manning, and Andrew Y Ng. 2010. Learning continuous phrase representations and syntactic parsing with recursive neural networks. In *Proceedings of the Advances in Neural Information Processing Systems 23 Deep Learning and Unsupervised Feature Learning Workshop*, pages 1–9.

Tijmen Tieleman and Geoffrey Hinton. 2012. Lecture 6.5-rmsprop: Divide the gradient by a running average of its recent magnitude. *COURSERA: Neural Networks for Machine Learning*, 4.

Kazushi Yoshida, Tomohiro Ohno, Yoshihide Kato, and Shigeki Matsubara. 2014. Japanese word reordering integrated with dependency parsing. In *Proceedings of COLING 2014, the 25th International Conference on Computational Linguistics: Technical Papers*.

Jiajun Zhang, Shujie Liu, Mu Li, Ming Zhou, and Chengqing Zong. 2014. Bilingually-constrained phrase embeddings for machine translation. In *Proceedings of the 52nd Annual Meeting of the Association for Computational Linguistics*.

Will Y. Zou, Richard Socher, Daniel Cer, and Christopher D. Manning. 2013. Bilingual word embeddings for phrase-based machine translation. In *Proceedings of the 2013 Conference on Empirical Methods in Natural Language Processing*.

The SAS Statistical Machine Translation System for WAT 2014

Rui Wang, Xu Yang and Yan Gao
SAS Institute Inc
Beijing, China
rui.wang|xu.yang|yan.gao@sas.com

Abstract

This paper is a description of the techniques and experiment results by SAS Institute Inc in WAT 2014 evaluation campaign. We participate in two subtasks of WAT 2014: the Chinese to Japanese track and the English to Japanese track. Our baseline system is MOSES statistical machine translation toolkit. We propose syntactic reordering approaches for English to Japanese and Chinese to Japanese translation which transform the order of source sentence into the target-like order. In addition, we apply the segmentation tool in SAS® Text Miner to enhance the translation results. Several contrastive experiments are presented based on the automatic evaluation results.

1 Introduction

This paper describes the machine translation system employed by SAS Institute Inc in the 1st Workshop on Asian Translation. We participate in two subtasks in this year's WAT evaluation campaign:

1) Chinese to Japanese;
2) English to Japanese.

We apply MOSES toolkit as the baseline system.

The sentence structure of Japanese is different with that of English and Chinese. Japanese is typically a Subject-Object-Verb (SOV) language while Chinese and English are Subject-Verb-Object (SVO) languages, as illustrated in Figure 1. The statistic machine translation between Japanese and the SVO language is particularly difficult because of the long distance difference of word orders. We propose a simple syntactic reordering approach for Chinese to Japanese and English to Japanese SMT in order to transform Chinese and English into SVO languages. Our submission mainly focuses on using the syntactic approaches to improve effectively improve the translation results. In addition, unlike the alphabetic languages, Chinese and Japanese need to be segmented into words of characters before translation. The accuracy of segmentation highly influences the performance of translation for Chinese and Japanese. We apply the tokenization tool in SAS® Text Miner to the corpus and obtain improvement of the translation results.

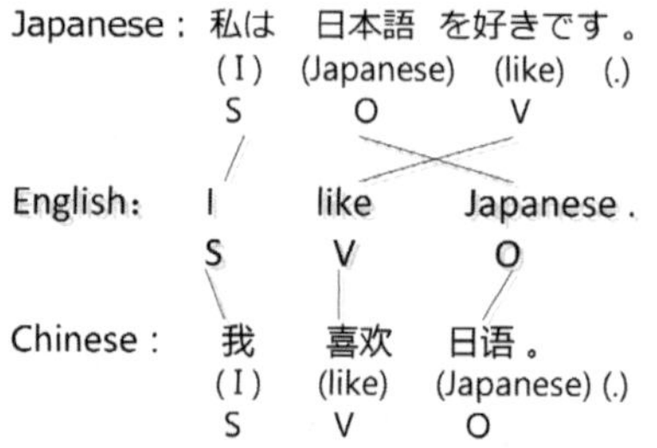

Figure 1: Word order differences of Japanese, Chinese and English.

The rest of this paper is organized as follows: in section 2 we describe the background; in section 3 we present the architecture of our system; Section 4 is the detailed description of the syntactic reordering rules we propose; experiment results are shown in section 5 and conclusion is made in section 6.

2 Background

The state of the art Statistical Machine Translation (SMT), phrase-based SMT (Koehn et al., 2003), works well on the translation between short phrases as well as on long sentences pairs with similar word orders. However the phrase-based SMT has limited capacity for long distance reordering since it does not consider the syntactic information in the translation. A great deal of recent research enhances the translation results by adding syntactic features, such syntactic-based SMT

Proceedings of the 1st Workshop on Asian Translation (WAT2014), pages 64–68,
Tokyo, Japan, 4th October 2014.

(Liu et al., 2006), or forest-based SMT (Mi et al., 2008). The language-independent methods parse the input sentences and then train reordering model from these parsed trees, such as Quirk et al. (2005), Li et al. (2007). These approaches improve the translation considerably but they are time consuming during decoding. Syntactic reordering approaches effectively improve the translation results by transforming the order of source-side language into target-like order.

Previous studies have proposed the syntactic reordering approach which is regarded as a preprocessing step on the source side language. Xia et al. (2004) automatically extract reordering rules on source side for English to French translation. Collins et al. (2005) improve the German to English translation by combining morphological and syntactical information into SMT system. Wang et al. (2007) extract the syntactic reordering rules manually on Chinese to English translation. Isozaki et al. (2010) propose a simple head finalized approach to reorder English into Japanese order based on Enju parser. We apply the head finalized method to our system and achieve improvement on the translation from English to Japanese. Dan et al. (2012) carry out a similar head finalized approach for Chinese to Japanese translation using a Chinese Enju parser (Yu et al., 2011). We propose a simple reordering methods for Chinese based on the accurate Berkeley Parser (Petrov et al., 2006).

3 System Architecture

We use the open-source SMT toolkit MOSES as the baseline to train translation model and to decode the test set for submission. SRILM (Stolcke et al. 2002) toolkit is applied to train the N-gram statistical language model. All the corpus are tokenized and lowercased before training and decoding. All the submitted results are detokenized. In addition to the basic phrase-based model, we also try hierarchical model (Chiang et al., 2007) using MOSES.

We use the segementation tool in SAS® Text Miner to tokenize Japanese and Chinese corpus

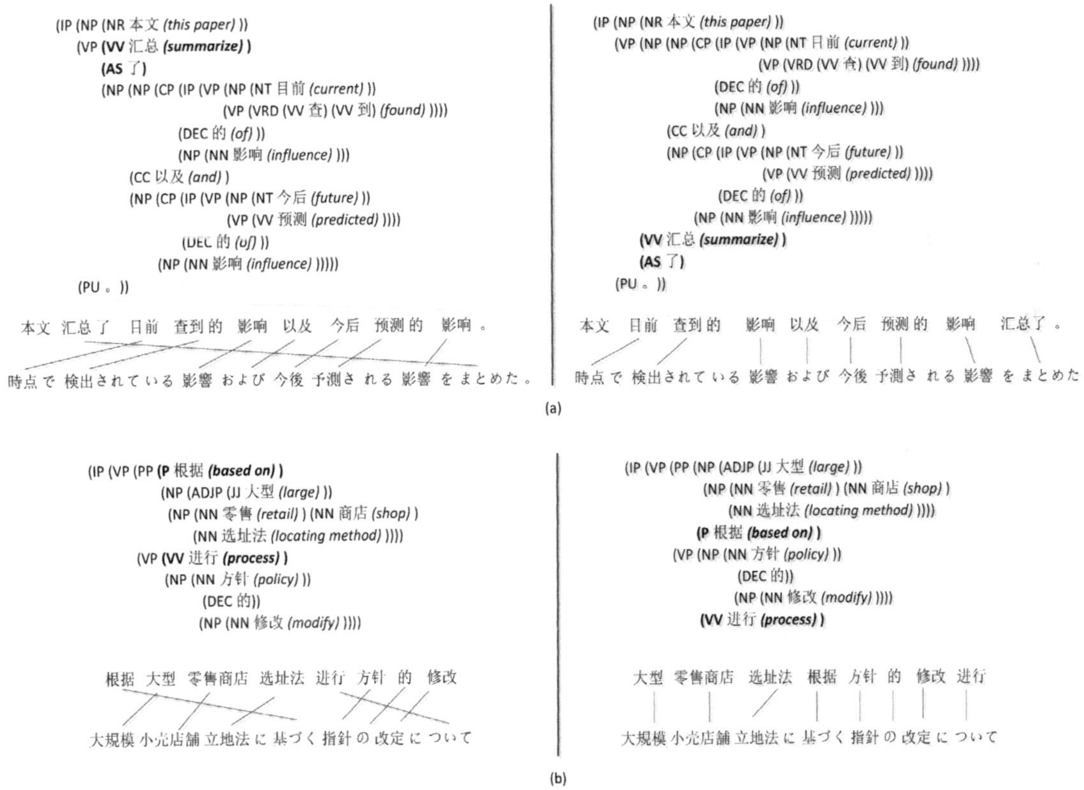

for training, tuning and testing. Then we use MOSES tool to lowercase the corpus and to clean long sentences. The syntactic reordering approach is applied on source-side cleaned sentences for English and Chinese. Finally the cleaned and reordered corpus is sent to MOSES to train models and decode results.

We use Berkeley parser (Petrov et al., 2006) to parse the source side Chinese sentence into syntactic tree and develop the reorder rules based on the grammatical structure of the sentence. English sentence is parsed by Enju parser and the head finalized reorder is applied as described by Isozaki et al. (2010).

4 Syntactic Reordering Approach

4.1 Chinese to Japanese reordering

The Chinese sentence is parsed into a grammatical tree using Pen Treebank syntactic tagset as illustrated in Figure 2. The main difference between Chinese and Japanese is the position of Verb Phrase (VP) and Prepositional Phrase (PP). We develop two simple reordering rules, VP-rule and PP-rule, based on the syntactic tree.

We develop the VP-rule, 'VP (VV AS (XXX)) →VP ((XXX) VV AS)', which means to move the verb (VV) and the auxiliary word (AS) behind VV to the end of the verb phrase (VP). For example, in Figure 2 (a), 'VV 汇总 (summarize)' and 'AS 了' are moved to the end of VP. The reordered Chinese sentence has more similar order with the Japanese translation than the original one.

The Preposition (P) is always at the end the Prepositional Phrase (PP) in Japanese while in Chinese P is located at the beginning of PP. We imply the PP-rule, 'PP (P (XXX)) → PP ((XXX) P)', to move P to the end of PP. In Figure 2 (b), the preposition '根据 (based on)' is move to the end of PP. The reordered sentence reduce the long distance order differences between the source Chinese and the target Japanese.

4.2 English to Japanese reordering

For English to Japanese translation, we use the head finalization approach proposed by Isozaki et al. (2010). In Japanese, the syntactic head word is located behind the dependent words while English is the opposite. The dependency parser, Enju parser, is applied on the source side which can output syntactic head, as illustrated in Figure 3. A simple reorder rule is defined: to move the syntactic head to the end of non-head words. In Figure 3, node C3 is the head of node C2. According to the head finalized reordering rule, C3 should be moved behind the other child of C2, C4. After reordering, the English sentence has the similar order with the Japanese sentence.

The head finalized reorder rule will reorder the coordination expressions such as, 'A and B', into 'B and A'. We add a coordination exception rule to stop reordering at coordination nodes.

5 Experiments

The experiment is conducted on the training data from ASPEC, consists of approximately 3 million

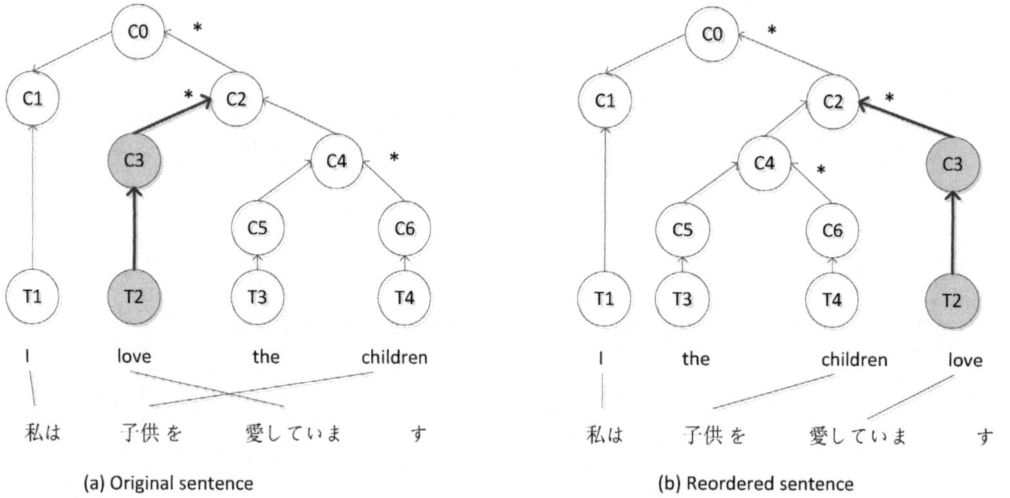

Figure 3: Example of reordering rules for English to Japanese translation. * represents the head of the node. (a) is the original sentence; (b) is the reordered sentence by head finalized rule.

Japanese-English parallel sentences and approximately 0.7 million Japanese-Chinese. BLEU and RIBES are used as evaluation metrics. On the evaluation websites, for Chinese to Japanese and English to Japanese evaluation, the results of BLEU and RIBES are measured under three Japanese segmentation tools: Juman, Kytea and Mecab. For the sake of brevity, we calculate the average score of the three segmentation tools for each evaluation metric.

5.1 Effect of the segmentation tool of SAS® Text Miner

We use phrase-based model as baseline for the Chinese to Japanese track to evaluate the effect of SAS segmentation tool. The result of baseline is provided by the WAT organizer (Toshiaki, et al. 2014). Table 1 shows that both the BLEU and RIBES are increased by using the segmentation tool of SAS® Text Miner for Chinese and Japanese corpus compared with the Juman segmentation tool for Japanese and Stanford Word Segmenter for Chinese. We conduct the other experiments using the segmentation tool of SAS® Text Miner because of its good performance.

	BLEU	RIBES
Baseline	34.86	0.769962
SAS segmentation	**35.31**	**0.809631**

Table 1: Effect of the segmentation tool of *SAS® Text Miner*.

5.2 Chinese to Japanese translation

	BLEU	RIBES
Baseline	34.86	0.769962
Baseline+VP	36.19	0.826146
Baseline+PP	36.30	0.815694
Baseline+PP+VP	36.40	0.826015
Hierarchical	36.06	0.814207
Hierarchical+PP+VP	**37.38**	**0.830909**

Table 2: Effect of reordering rules for Chinese to Japanese translation.

Table 2 shows the effect of reordering rules for Chinese to Japanese translation. The baseline is the results from the WAT organizer (Toshiaki, et al. 2014). We propose two reordering rules: VP rule and PP rule. The baseline is the phrase-based machine translation using MOSES. We apply the VP rule, PP rule and the combination of the two rules to the corpus separately and send the reordered sentences to the baseline system. Both the VP rule and PP rule have contribution to the improvement of BLEU scores. We also apply the reorder rules to the hierarchical model and gain 2.07 in BLEU scores compared with the baseline system.

5.3 English to Japanese translation

The effect of the head finalized reordering rule for English to Japanese translation is reported in Table 3. The phrase-based model is applied as baseline system. After head finalized reordering, the BLEU score is increased from 28.52 by the organizer (Toshiaki, et al. 2014) to 31.09. We gain 3.13 in BLEU score by applying the hierarchical model with pre-reordering.

	BLEU	RIBES
Baseline	28.52	0.690350
Baseline+reorder	31.09	0.765005
Hierarchical	31.23	0.743135
Hierarchical+reorder	**31.65**	**0.767323**

Table 3: Effect of the head finalized reordering rule for English to Japanese translation.

6 Conclusion

This paper describes the techniques and experiment results in WAT 2014 evaluation campaign submitted by SAS Institute Inc. By applying the tokenization tool in SAS® Text Miner and the syntactic reordering rules, we achieve significant improvements on Chinese to Japanese translation and English to Japanese translation. We also report some extensive experiment results to illustrate the contribution on different parts.

In the future, we intend to consider case markers in Japanese which other languages do not have. Since the form of Japanese case markers is known, we may define rules to insert particular tags to the source languages. We expect improvements of translation by adding the rules of case markers in Japanese.

Reference

Koehn, Philipp, Franz Josef Och, and Daniel Marcu. 2003. "Statistical phrase-based translation." *Proceedings of the 2003 Conference of the North American Chapter of the Association for Computational Linguistics on Human Language Technology-Volume 1*. Association for Computational Linguistics.

Liu, Yang, Qun Liu, and Shouxun Lin. 2006. "Tree-to-string alignment template for statistical machine translation." *Proceedings of the 21st International Conference on Computational Linguistics and the*

44th annual meeting of the Association for Computational Linguistics.

Mi, Haitao, Liang Huang, and Qun Liu. 2008. "Forest-Based Translation." *ACL.*

Quirk, Chris, Arul Menezes, and Colin Cherry. 2005. "Dependency treelet translation: Syntactically informed phrasal SMT." *Proceedings of the 43rd Annual Meeting on Association for Computational Linguistics.*

Li, Chi-Ho, et al. 2007. "A probabilistic approach to syntax-based reordering for statistical machine translation." *ANNUAL MEETING-ASSOCIATION FOR COMPUTATIONAL LINGUISTICS. Vol. 45. No. 1.*

Xia, Fei, and Michael McCord. 2004. "Improving a statistical MT system with automatically learned rewrite patterns." *Proceedings of the 20th international conference on Computational Linguistics.* Association for Computational Linguistics.

Collins, Michael, Philipp Koehn, and Ivona Kučerová. 2005. "Clause restructuring for statistical machine translation." *Proceedings of the 43rd annual meeting on association for computational linguistics.* Association for Computational Linguistics.

Wang, Chao, Michael Collins, and Philipp Koehn. 2007. "Chinese Syntactic Reordering for Statistical Machine Translation." *EMNLP-CoNLL.*

Isozaki, Hideki, et al. 2010. "Head finalization: A simple reordering rule for sov languages." *Proceedings of the Joint Fifth Workshop on Statistical Machine Translation and MetricsMATR.* Association for Computational Linguistics.

Dan, Han, et al. 2012. "Head finalization reordering for Chinese-to-Japanese machine translation." *Proceedings of the Sixth Workshop on Syntax, Semantics and Structure in Statistical Translation.* Association for Computational Linguistics.

Yu, Kun, et al. 2011. "Analysis of the difficulties in Chinese deep parsing."*Proceedings of the 12th International Conference on Parsing Technologies.* Association for Computational Linguistics.

Stolcke, Andreas. 2002. "SRILM-an extensible language modeling toolkit."*INTERSPEECH.*

Chiang, David. 2007. "Hierarchical phrase-based translation." *computational linguistics* 33.2: 201-228.

Petrov, Slav, et al. 2006. "Learning accurate, compact, and interpretable tree annotation." *Proceedings of the 21st International Conference on Computational Linguistics and the 44th annual meeting of the Association for Computational Linguistics.* Association for Computational Linguistics.

Toshiaki Nakazawa, et al. 2014. "Overview of the 1st Workshop on Asian Translation". Proceedings of the 1st Workshop on Asian Translation (WAT2014)

Consistent Improvement in Translation Quality of Chinese–Japanese Technical Texts by Adding Additional Quasi-parallel Training Data

Wei Yang
Graduate School of IPS
Waseda University
2-7 Hibikino, Wakamatsu-ku
Kitakyushu, Fukuoka 808-0135, Japan
kevinyoogi@akane.waseda.ja

Yves Lepage
Graduate School of IPS
Waseda University
2-7 Hibikino, Wakamatsu-ku
Kitakyushu, Fukuoka 808-0135, Japan
yves.lepage@waseda.ja

Abstract

Bilingual parallel corpora are an extremely important resource as they are typically used in data-driven machine translation. There already exist many freely available corpora for European languages, but almost none between Chinese and Japanese. The constitution of large bilingual corpora is a problem for less documented language pairs. We construct a quasi-parallel corpus automatically by using analogical associations based on certain number of parallel corpus and a small number of monolingual data. Furthermore, in SMT experiments performed on Chinese-Japanese, by adding this kind of data into the baseline training corpus, on the same test set, the evaluation scores of the translation results we obtained were significantly or slightly improved over the baseline systems.

1 Introduction

Bilingual corpora are an essential resource for current SMT. So as to enlarge such corpora, technology research has been done in extracting parallel sentences from existing non-parallel corpora. The approaches and difficulties depend on the parallelness of the given bilingual parallel corpus. Fung and Cheung (2004) give a detailed description of the types of non-parallel corpora. They proposed a completely unsupervised method for mining parallel sentences from quasi-comparable bilingual texts which include both in-topic and off-topic documents. Chu et al. (2013) proposed a novel method of classifier training and testing that simulates the real parallel sentence extraction process. They used linguistic knowledge of Chinese character features. Their approach improved in several aspects and worked well for extracting parallel sentences from quasi–comparable corpora. Their experimental results on parallel sentence extraction from quasi–comparable corpora indicated that their proposed system performs significantly better than previous studies.

There also exist some works on extracting parallel parallel sentences from comparable corpora, such as Wikipedia. Smith et al. (2010) include features which make use of the additional annotation given by Wikipedia, and features using an automatically induced lexicon model.

In this paper, we propose to construct a bilingual corpus of quasi-parallel sentences automatically. This is different from parallel or comparable or quasi-comparable corpora. A quasi-parallel corpus contains aligned sentence pairs that are translations to each other to a certain extent. The method relies on a certain number of existing parallel sentences and a small number of unaligned, unrelated, monolingual sentences. To construct the quasi-parallel corpus, analogical associations captured by analogical clusters are used. The motivation is that the construction of large bilingual corpora is a problem for less-resourced language pairs, but it is to be noticed that the monolingual data are easier to access in large amounts. The languages that we tackle in this paper are: Chinese and Japanese.

Our approach leverages Chinese and Japanese monolingual data collected from the Web by clustering and grouping these sentences using analogical associations. Our clusters can be considered as rewriting models for new sentence generation. We generate new sentences using these rewriting models starting from seed sentences from the monolingual part of the existing parallel corpus we used, and filter out dubious newly over-generated sentences. Finally, we extract newly generated sentences and assess the strength of translation relations between them based on the similarity, across languages, between the clusters they were generated from.

Proceedings of the 1st Workshop on Asian Translation (WAT2014), pages 69–76,
Tokyo, Japan, 4th October 2014.

2 Chinese and Japanese Linguistic Resources

2.1 Chinese and Japanese Parallel Sentences

The Chinese and Japanese linguistic resources we use in this paper are the ASPEC-JC[1] corpus. It is a parallel corpus consisting of Japanese scientific papers from the reference database and electronic journal site J-STAGE of the Japan Science and Technology Agency (JST) that have been translated to Chinese after receiving permission from the necessary academic associations. The parts selected were abstracts and paragraph units from the body text, as these contain the highest overall vocabulary coverage.

This corpus is designed for Machine Translation and is split as below (some statistics are given in Table 1):

- Training Data: 672,315 sentences;
- Development Data: 2,090 sentences;
- Development-Test Data: 2,148 sentences;
- Test Data: 2,107 sentences.

For new sentence generation from the training data, we extracted 103,629 Chinese-Japanese parallel sentences with less than 30 characters in length. We propose to make use of this part of data as seed sentences for new sentence generation in both languages, then deduce and construct a Chinese—Japanese quasi-parallel corpus that we will use as additional data to inflate the baseline training corpus.

2.2 Chinese and Japanese Monolingual Sentences

To generate new quasi-parallel data, we also use unrelated unaligned monolingual data. We collected monolingual Chinese and Japanese short sentences with less than 30 characters in size from the Web using an in-house Web-crawler, mainly from the following websites: "Yahoo China", "Yahoo China News", "douban" for Chinese and "Yahoo! JAPAN", "Mainichi Japan" for Japanese. Table 2 gives the statistics of the cleaned 70,000 monolingual data that we used in the experiments.

[1] `http://orchid.kuee.kyoto-u.ac.jp/ASPEC/`

3 Constructing Analogical Clusters According to Proportional Analogies

3.1 Proportional Analogies

Proportional analogies establish a structural relationship between four objects, A, B, C and D: 'A is to B as C is to D'. An efficient algorithm for the resolution of analogical equations between strings of characters has been proposed in (Lepage, 1998).

The algorithm relies on counting numbers of occurrences of characters and computing edit distances (with only insertion and deletion as edit operations) between strings of characters ($d(A,B) = d(C,D)$ and $d(A,C) = d(B,D)$). The algorithm uses fast bit string operations and distance computation (Allison and Dix, 1986).

3.1.1 Sentential Analogies

We gather pairs of sentences that constitute proportional analogies, independently in Chinese and Japanese. For instance, the two following pairs of Japanese sentences are said to form an analogy, because the edit distance between the sentence pair on the left of '::' is the same as between the sentence pair on the right side: $d(A,B) = d(C,D) = 13$ and $d(A,C) = d(B,D) = 5$, and the relation on the number of occurrences of characters, which must be valid for each character, may be illustrated as follows for the character 茶: 1 (in A) - 1 (in B) = 0 (in C) - 0 (in D). We call any such two pairs of sentences a *sentential analogy*.

紅茶が飲みたい。	:	あなたは紅茶が好きですか。	::	ビールが飲みたい。	:	あなたはビールが好きですか。
I'd like a cup of black tea.	:	*Do you like black tea?*	::	*I'd like a beer.*	:	*Do you like beer?*

3.1.2 Analogical Cluster

When several sentential analogies involve the same pairs of sentences, they form a series of analogous sentences, and they can be written on a sequence of lines where each line contains one sentence pair and where any two pairs of sentences from the sequence of lines forms a *sentential analogy*. We call such a sequence of lines an *analogical cluster*. The size of a cluster is the number of its sentential pairs. The following example in Japanese shows three possible sentential analogies and the size of the cluster is 3. English translation is given below.

ASPEC-JC	Language	# of different sentences	size of sentences in characters mean ± std.dev.	total characters	total words	voc. size
	Chinese	668,942	46.93 ± 26.62	31,462,440	18,847,514	295,580
	Japanese	666,938	59.69 ± 32.05	39,987,827	23,480,703	145,074

Table 1: Statistics on the ASPEC Chinese–Japanese corpus used for training (672,315 sentences). Segmentation tools: urheen for Chinese and mecab for Japanese.

	# of different sentences (cleaned)	size of sentences in characters (mean ± std.dev.)	total characters	total words
Chinese	70,000	10.29 ± 6.21	775,530	525,462
Japanese	70,000	15.06 ± 6.34	1,139,588	765,085

Table 2: Statistics on the cleaned Chinese and Japanese monolingual short sentences. Segmentation tools: urheen for Chinese and mecab for Japanese.

紅茶が飲みたい。	:	あなたは紅茶が好きですか。
ビールが飲みたい。	:	あなたはビールが好きですか。
ジュースが飲みたい。	:	あなたはジュースが好きですか。

I'd like a cup of black tea.	:	*Do you like black tea?*
I'd like a beer.	:	*Do you like beer?*
I'd like some juice.	:	*Do you like juice?*

As we will see in Section 4, analogical clusters can be considered as *rewriting models*. New sentences can be generated using them.

3.2 Experiments on clusters production

In each language, independently, we also construct analogical clusters from the unrelated monolingual data. The number of unique sentences used is 70,000 for both languages. Table 3 summarizes some statistics on the clusters produced.

	Chinese	Japanese
# of different sentences	70,000	70,000
# of clusters	23,182	21,975

Table 3: Statistics on the Chinese and Japanese clusters constructed from our unrelated monolingual data independently in each language.

3.3 Determining corresponding clusters by computing similarity

The steps for determining corresponding clusters are,

- First, for each sentence pair in a cluster, we extract the change between the left and the right sides by finding the longest common subsequence (LCS) (Wagner and Fischer, 1974).
- Then, we consider the changes between the left (S_{left}) and the right (S_{right}) sides in one cluster as two sets. We perform word segmentation[2] on these changes in sets to obtain minimal sets of changes made up with words or characters.
- Finally, we compute the similarity between the left sets (S_{left}) and the right sets (S_{right}) of Chinese and Japanese clusters. To this end, we make use of the EDR dictionary[3] and word-to-word alignments (based on ASPEC-JC data using Anymalign[4]), We keep 72,610 word-to-word correspondences obtained with

[2] Segmentation toolkits: Mecab, Part-of-Speech and Morphological Analyzer: `http://mecab.googlecode.com/svn/trunk/mecab/doc/index.html` for Japanese and Urheen, a Chinese lexical analysis toolkit (National Laboratory of Pattern Recognition, China) for Chinese.

[3] `http://www2.nict.go.jp/out-promotion/techtransfer/EDR/index.html`

[4] `http://anymalign.limsi.fr`

Anymalign in 1 hour after filtering on both translation probabilities with a threshold of 0.3, the quality of these word-to-word correspondences is about 96%. We also use a traditional-simplified Chinese variant table[5] and Kanji-Hanzi Conversion Table[6] to translate all Japanese words into Chinese, or convert Japanese characters into simplified Chinese characters. We calculate the similarity between two Chinese and Japanese word sets according to a classical Dice formula:

$$Sim = \frac{2 \times |S_{zh} \cap S_{ja}|}{|S_{zh}| + |S_{ja}|} \qquad (1)$$

Here, S_{zh} and S_{ja} denote the minimal sets of changes across the clusters (both on the left or right) in both languages (after translation and conversion). To compute the similarity between two Chinese and Japanese clusters we take the arithmetic mean on both sides, as given in formula (2):

$$Sim_{C_{zh}-C_{ja}} = \frac{1}{2}(Sim_{left} + Sim_{right}) \qquad (2)$$

We set different thresholds for $Sim_{C_{zh}-C_{ja}}$ and check the correspondence between these extracted clusters by sampling. Where the $Sim_{C_{zh}-C_{ja}}$ threshold is set to 0.300, the acceptability of the correspondence between the extracted clusters reaches 78%. About 15,710 corresponding clusters were extracted ($Sim_{C_{zh}-C_{ja}} \geq 0.300$) by the above steps.

4 Generating New Sentences Using Analogical Associations

4.1 Generation of New Sentences

Analogy is not only a structural relationship. It is also a process (Itkonen, 2005) by which, "given two related forms and only one form, the fourth missing form is coined" (de Saussure, 1916). If the objects *A*, *B*, *C* are given, we may obtain an other unknown object *D* according to the analogical equation *A* : *B* :: *C* : *D*. This principle can be illustrated as follows with sentences:

紅茶が飲みたい。 : あなたは紅茶が好きですか。 :: ビールが飲みたい。 : x

⇒ x = あなたはビールが好きですか。

[5]http://www.unicode.org/Public/UNIDATA/

[6]http://www.kishugiken.co.jp/cn/code10d.html

In this example, the solution of the analogical equation is *D* = "あなたはビールが好きですか。" (Do you like beer?). If we regard each sentence pair in a cluster as a pair *A* : *B* (left to right or right to left), and any short sentence not belonging to the cluster as *C* (a *seed sentence*), the analogical equation *A* : *B* :: *C* : *D* of unknown *D* can be forged. Such analogical equations allow us to produce new candidate sentences. Each sentence pair in a cluster is a potential template for the generation of new candidate sentences.

4.2 Experiments on New Sentences Generation and Filtering by N-sequences

For the generation of new sentences, we make use of the clusters we obtained from the experiments in Section 3.2 as *rewriting models*. The seed sentences as input data for new sentences generation are the unique Chinese and Japanese short sentences from the 103,629 ASPEC-JC parallel sentences (less than 30 characters). In this experiment, we generated new sentences with each pair of sentences in clusters for Chinese and Japanese respectively. Table 4 gives the statistics for new sentence generation.

To filter out invalid and grammatically incorrect sentences and keep only well-formed sentences with high fluency of expression and adequacy of meaning, we eliminate any sentence that contains an N-sequence of a given length unseen in the reference corpus. This technique to assess the quality of outputs of NLP systems has been used in previous works (Lin and Hovy, 2003; Doddington, 2002; Lepage and Denoual, 2005). In our experiment, we introduced begin/end markers to make sure that the beginning and the end of a sentence are also correct. The best quality was obtained for the values N=6 for Chinese and N=7 for Japanese with the size of reference corpus (about 1,700,000 monolingual data for both Chinese and Japanese). Quality assessment was performed by extracting a sample of 1,000 sentences randomly and checking manually by native speakers. The grammatical quality was at least 96%. This means that 96% of the Chinese and Japanese sentences may be considered as grammatically correct. For new valid sentences, we remember their corresponding seed sentences and the cluster they were generated from.

		Chinese		Japanese	
Initial data	# of seed sentences	99,538		97,152	
	# of clusters	23,182		21,975	
New sentence generation	# of candidate sentences	105,038,200 Q= 29%		80,183,424 Q= 40%	
Quality assessment (filtered)	# of new valid sentences	unique	seed–new–#	unique	seed–new–#
		33,141	67,099	40,234	84,533
		Q= 96%		Q= 96%	

Table 4: Statistics on new sentence generation in Chinese and Japanese. Q is the quality of the new candidate sentences or new valid sentences after filtering.

Chinese	Japanese	Chinese–Japanese		
seed–new–#	seed–new–#	Initial parallel corpus	Corresponding clusters	Quasi-parallel corpus
67,099	84,533	103,629	15,710	35,817

Table 5: Statistics on the quasi-parallel corpus deducing.

4.3 Deducing and Acquiring Quasi-parallel Sentences

We deduce translation relations based on the initial parallel corpus and corresponding clusters between Chinese and Japanese. If the seeds of two new generated sentences in Chinese and Japanese are aligned in the initial parallel corpus, and if the clusters which they were generated from are corresponding, we suppose that these two Chinese and Japanese newly generated sentences are translations of one another to a certain extent. Table 5 gives the statistics on the quasi-parallel deducing obtained. Among the 35,817 unique Chinese–Japanese quasi-parallel sentences obtained, about 74% were found to be exact translations by manual check on a sampling of 1,000 pairs of sentences. This justifies our use of the term "quasi-parallel" for this kind of data.

5 SMT Experiments

5.1 Experimental Protocol

To assess the contribution of the generated quasi-parallel corpus, we propose to compare two SMT systems. The first one is constructed using the initial given ASPEC-JC parallel corpus. This is the baseline. The second one adds the additional quasi-parallel corpus obtained using analogical associations and analogical clusters.

Baseline: The statistics of the data used in the experiments are given in Table 6 (left). The training corpus consists of 672,315 sentences of initial Chinese–Japanese parallel corpus. The tuning set is 2,090 sentences from the ASPEC-JC.dev corpus, and 2,107 sentences also from the ASPEC-JC.test corpus were used for testing. We perform all experiments using the standard GIZA++/MOSES pipeline (Och and Ney, 2003).

Adding Additional Quasi-parallel Corpus: The statistics of the data used in this second setting are given in Table 6 (right). The training corpus is made of 708,132 (672,315 + 35,817) sentences, i.e., the combination of the initial Chinese–Japanese parallel corpus used in the baseline and the quasi-parallel corpus.

Experimental Results: Table 7 and Table 8 give the evaluation results. We use the standard metrics BLEU (Papineni et al., 2002), NIST (Doddington et al., 2000), WER (Nießen et al., 2000), TER (Snover et al., 2006) and RIBES (Isozaki et al., 2010). As Table 7 shows, significant improvement over the baseline is obtained by adding the quasi-parallel generated data based on the Moses version 1.0, and Table 8 shows a slightly improvement over the baseline is obtained by adding the quasi-parallel generated data based on the Moses version 2.1.1.

5.2 Influence of Segmentation on Translation Results

We also use Kytea[7] to segment Chinese and Japanese. Table 9 and Table 10 show the evaluation results by using Kytea as the segmentation

[7] http://www.phontron.com/kytea/index-ja.html

tools based on standard GIZA++/MOSES (different version in 1.0 and 2.1.1) pipeline. As the evaluation scores (BLEU and RIBES) shown in Table 7, Table 8, Table 9 and Table 10:

- We obtained more increase based on Moses version 1.0 than Moses version 2.1.1 by using urheen/mecab or kytea for Chinese and Japanese as the segmentation tools;
- But, based on Moses version 2.1.1 we obtained higher BLEU and RIBES than Moses version 1.0 by using two different segmentation tools;
- Based on the same Moses version, most of the BLEU and RIBES scores are higher by using urheen and mecab as the segmentation tools for Chinese and Japanese than using kytea (except ja-zh by using kytea based on Moses version 2.1.1).

5.3 Issues for Context-aware Machine Translation

Context-aware plays an important role in disambiguation and machine translation. Usually, the MT systems look at surface form only, conversational speech tends to be more concise and more context-dependent (Example1), and some ambiguities often arises due to polysemy (Example2 from our experiment results by using urheen and mecab as the segmentation tools) and homonymy.

Example1: 下次我要尝尝白的。

Reference_en: I'll try Chinese **wine** next time.

Reference_ja: 今度は中国のワインを試してみます。

MT output_en: Next time I'll try the **white**.

MT output_ja: 次回は私は白を試してみます。

Example2: 结果发现，其中昼夜均符合环境标准的地点是，平成１５年度为６３处（３６．２％），平成１６年度为５９处（３７．８％）。

Reference_ja: その結果，全地点のうち昼夜ともに環境基準地を達成したのは，平成１５年度の６３地点（３６．２％），平成１６年度で５９地点（３７．８％）であった。

MT output (google): それは、昼と夜が環境基準に沿ったものである場所が63（36.2％）が平成15年であることが判明した、平成59（37.8％）が16歳。

MT output (our base-line): その結果，その昼夜ともに環境基準の地点は，平成１５年度は６３箇所（３６．２％）では，平成１６年度は５９箇所（３７．８％）であった。

MT output (our base-line+add): その結果，その昼夜ともに環境基準の地点は，平成１５年度は６３箇所（３６．２％）では，平成１６年度は５９箇所（３７．８％）であった。

As the Example2 shows, we obtained the better and more correct translation results based on our translation systems. Correct meaning of a word or a sentence depends context information. The large training data in the same domain is also an extremely important factor in translation systems. They allow us to obtain the well-formed translation result with high fluency of expression and adequacy of meaning.

6 Conclusion

We presented a technique to automatically generate a quasi-parallel corpus to inflate the training corpus used to build an SMT system. The experimental data we use are ASPEC-JC corpus and the monolingual data were collected from the Web. We produced analogical clusters as rewriting models to generate new sentences, and filter newly over-generated sentences by the N-sequences filtering method. The grammatical quality of the valid new sentences is at least 96%. We then assess translation relations between newly generated short sentences across both languages, relying on the similarity between the clusters across languages. We automatically obtained 35,817 Chinese–Japanese sentence pairs, 74% of which were found to be exact translations. We call such sentence pairs a quasi-parallel corpus.

In SMT experiments performed on Chinese–Japanese, using the standard GIZA++/MOSES pipeline, by adding our quasi-parallel data, we were able to inflate the training data in a rewarding way. On the same test set, based on different MOSES versions and segmentation tools, all of translation scores significantly or slightly improved over the baseline systems. It should be stressed that the data that allowed us to get such improvement are not so large in quantity and not so good in quality, but we were able to control both quantity and quality so as to consistently improve translation quality.

Acknowledgments

This work was supported in part by Foreign Joint Project funds from the Kitakyushu Foundation for the Advancement of Industry, Science and Technology (FAIS).

References

Lloyd Allison and Trevor I. Dix. 1986. A bit string longest common subsequence algorithm. *Information Processing Letter*, 23:305–310.

Chenhui Chu, Toshiaki Nakazawa, and Sadao Kurohashi. 2013. Chinese–Japanese parallel sentence extraction from quasi–comparable corpora. In *ACL 2013*, pages 34–42.

Ferdinand de Saussure. 1916. *Cours de linguistique générale*. Payot, Lausanne et Paris, [1ère éd. 1916] edition.

George R Doddington, Mark A Przybocki, Alvin F Martin, and Douglas A Reynolds. 2000. The NIST speaker recognition evaluation–overview, methodology, systems, results, perspective. *Speech Communication*, 31(2):225–254.

George Doddington. 2002. Automatic evaluation of machine translation quality using n-gram cooccurrence statistics. In *Proceedings of the Human Language Technology Conference (HLT2002)*, pages 128–132, San Diego, CA, USA. Morgan Kaufmann.

Pascale Fung and Percy Cheung. 2004. Multilevel bootstrapping for extracting parallel sentences from a quasi-comparable corpus. In *In COLING 2004*, pages 1051–1057.

Hideki Isozaki, Tsutomu Hirao, Kevin Duh, Katsuhito Sudoh, and Hajime Tsukada. 2010. Automatic evaluation of translation quality for distant language pairs. In *Proceedings of the 2010 Conference on Empirical Methods in Natural Language Processing*, pages 944–952. Association for Computational Linguistics.

Esa Itkonen. 2005. *Analogy as Structure and Process: Approaches in linguistics, cognitive psychology and philosophy of science*, volume 14.

Yves Lepage and Etienne Denoual. 2005. Automatic generation of paraphrases to be used as translation references in objective evaluation measures of machine translation. In *IWP2005*, pages 57–64.

Yves Lepage. 1998. Solving analogies on words: An algorithm. In *Proceedings of COLING-ACL'98*, pages 728–735, Montréal, August.

Chin-Yew Lin and Eduard Hovy. 2003. Automatic evaluation of summaries using n-gram cooccurrence statistics. In *Proceedings of the 2003 Conference of the North American Chapter of the Association for Computational Linguistics on Human Language Technology (HLT-NAACL-2003)*, pages 71–78.

Toshiaki Nakazawa, Hideya Mino, Isao Goto, Sadao Kurohashi, and Eiichiro Sumita. 2014. Overview of the 1st workshop on asian translation. In *Proceedings of the 1st Workshop on Asian Translation (WAT2014)*.

Sonja Nießen, Franz Josef Och, Gregor Leusch, and Hermann Ney. 2000. An evaluation tool for machine translation: Fast evaluation for machine translation research. In *Proceedings of LREC '00*, pages 39–45.

Franz Josef Och and Hermann Ney. 2003. A systematic comparison of various statistical alignment models. *Computational Linguistics*, 29(1):19–51.

Kishore Papineni, Salim Roukos, Todd Ward, and Wei-Jing Zhu. 2002. BLEU: a method for automatic evaluation of machine translation. In *ACL 2002*, pages 311–318.

Jason R Smith, Chris Quirk, and Kristina Toutanova. 2010. Extracting parallel sentences from comparable corpora using document level alignment. In *Human Language Technologies: The 2010 Annual Conference of the North American Chapter of the Association for Computational Linguistics*, pages 403–411. Association for Computational Linguistics.

Matthew Snover, Bonnie Dorr, Richard Schwartz, Linnea Micciulla, and John Makhoul. 2006. A study of translation edit rate with targeted human annotation. In *AMTA '06*, pages 223–231.

Robert A. Wagner and Michael J. Fischer. 1974. The string-to-string correction problem. *Journal of the ACM*, 21:168–173.

	Baseline	Chinese	Japanese
train	sentences	672,315	672,315
	words	18,847,514	23,480,703
	mean ± std.dev.	28.12 ± 15.20	35.05 ± 18.88

	+ Quasi-parallel	Chinese	Japanese
train	sentences	**708,132**	**708,132**
	words	19,212,187	24,512,079
	mean ± std.dev.	27.13 ± 14.19	34.23 ± 17.22

	Both experiments	Chinese	Japanese
tune	sentences	2,090	2,090
	words	60,458	73,177
	mean ± std.dev.	28.93 ± 15.86	35.01 ± 18.87
test	sentences	2,107	2,107
	words	59,594	72,027
	mean ± std.dev.	28.28 ± 14.55	34.18 ± 17.43

Table 6: Statistics on the Chinese–Japanese corpus used for the training, tuning, and test sets in baseline (left) and baseline + quasi-parallel data (right). The tuning and testing sets are the same in both experiments. Segmentation tools: urheen for Chinese and Mecab for Japanese.

		BLEU	NIST	WER	TER	RIBES
zh-ja	baseline	29.10	7.5677	0.5352	0.5478	0.7801
	+ additional training data	**32.03**	**7.9741**	**0.5069**	**0.5172**	**0.7906**
ja-zh	baseline	22.98	7.0103	0.5481	0.5711	0.7893
	+ additional training data	**24.87**	**7.3208**	**0.5273**	**0.5482**	**0.8013**

Table 7: Evaluation results for Chinese–Japanese translation across two SMT systems (baseline and baseline + additional quasi-parallel data), Moses version: 1.0, segmentation tools: urheen and mecab.

		BLEU	NIST	WER	TER	RIBES
zh-ja	baseline	33.41	8.1537	0.4967	0.5061	0.7956
	+ additional training data	**33.68**	**8.1820**	**0.4955**	**0.5039**	**0.7964**
ja-zh	baseline	25.53	7.3885	0.5227	0.5427	0.8053
	+ additional training data	**25.80**	**7.4571**	**0.5176**	**0.5378**	**0.8060**

Table 8: Evaluation results for Chinese–Japanese translation across two SMT systems (baseline and baseline + additional quasi-parallel data), Moses version: 2.1.1, segmentation tools: Urheen and Mecab.

		BLEU	NIST	WER	TER	RIBES
zh-ja	baseline	28.35	7.3123	0.5667	0.5741	0.7610
	+ additional training data	**28.87**	**7.4637**	**0.5566**	**0.5615**	**0.7739**
ja-zh	baseline	22.83	6.9533	0.5633	0.5853	0.7807
	+ additional training data	**23.18**	**7.0402**	**0.5547**	**0.5778**	**0.7865**

Table 9: Evaluation results for Chinese–Japanese translation across two SMT systems (baseline and baseline + additional quasi-parallel data), Moses version:1.0, segmentation tools: Kytea.

		BLEU	NIST	WER	TER	RIBES
zh-ja	baseline	33.27	7.9579	0.5249	0.5272	0.7820
	+ additional training data	**33.56**	**8.0229**	**0.5178**	**0.5206**	**0.7849**
ja-zh	baseline	26.25	7.4931	0.5197	0.5398	0.8085
	+ additional training data	**26.52**	**7.5523**	**0.5128**	**0.5335**	**0.8105**

Table 10: Evaluation results for Chinese–Japanese translation across two SMT systems (baseline and baseline + additional quasi-parallel data), Moses version: 2.1.1, segmentation tools: Kytea.

Word Order Does NOT Differ Significantly Between Chinese and Japanese

Chenchen Ding[†‡•] **Masao Utiyama**[†∘] **Eiichiro Sumita**[†∘] **Mikio Yamamoto**[‡•]
[†]Multilingual Translation Laboratory,
National Institute of Information and Communications Technology
3-5 Hikaridai, Seikacho, Sorakugun, Kyoto, 619-0289, Japan
[‡]Department of Computer Science, University of Tsukuba
1-1-1 Tennodai, Tsukuba, Ibaraki, 305-8573, Japan
•{tei@mibel., myama@}cs.tsukuba.ac.jp
∘{mutiyama, eiichiro.sumita}@nict.go.jp

Abstract

We propose a pre-reordering approach for Japanese-to-Chinese statistical machine translation (SMT). The approach uses dependency structure and manually designed reordering rules to arrange morphemes of Japanese sentences into Chinese-like word order, before a baseline phrase-based (PB) SMT system applied. Experimental results on the ASPEC-JC data show that the improvement of the proposed pre-reordering approach is slight on BLEU and mediocre on RIBES, compared with the organizer's baseline PB SMT system. The approach also shows improvement in human evaluation. We observe the word order does not differ much in the two languages, though Japanese is a subject-object-verb (SOV) language and Chinese is an SVO language.

1 Introduction

The state-of-the-art techniques of statistical machine translation (SMT) (Koehn et al., 2003; Koehn et al., 2007) demonstrate good performance on translation of languages with relatively similar word orders (Koehn, 2005). However, word reordering is a problematic issue for language pairs with significantly different word orders, such as the translation between a subject-verb-object (SVO) language and a subject-object-verb (SOV) language (Isozaki et al., 2012).

To resolve the word reordering problem in SMT, a line of research handles the word reordering as a separate pre-process, which is referred as *pre-reordering*. In pre-reordering, the word order on source-side is arranged into the target-side word order, before a standard SMT system is applied, on both training and decoding phases.

An effective rule-based approach, *head finalization* has been proposed for English-to-Japanese translation (Isozaki et al., 2012). The approach takes advantage of the *head final* property of Japanese on the target-side. It designs a head finalization rule to move the head word based on the parsing result by a head-driven phrase structure grammar (HPSG) parser. Generally, the idea can be applied to other SVO-to-Japanese translation tasks, such as its application in Chinese-to-Japanese translation (Dan et al., 2012).

However, the head finalization cannot be applied on the reverse translation task, i.e. Japanese-to-SVO translation, which becomes a more difficult task. Specifically, Japanese-to-English translation has been studied and several rule-based pre-reordering approaches have been proposed, taking advantage of the characters of Japanese and English (Komachi et al., 2006; Katz-Brown and Collins, 2008; Sudoh et al., 2011; Hoshino et al., 2013; Ding et al., 2014). A comparison of these approaches is reported in Ding et al. (2014).

Because both Chinese and English are SVO languages, to transfer approaches of Japanese-to-English to Japanese-to-Chinese translation is a natural idea. Based on the framework of Ding et al. (2014), we propose dependency-based pre-reordering rules for Japanese-to-Chinese translation in this paper. Contrary to our expectations, from the experimental results on ASPEC-JC data, we discover that the rule-based pre-reordering cannot improve the Japanese-to-Chinese significantly as in the case of Japanese-to-English translation. In a further investigation, we find a basic reason is that the word order is actually similar between Chinese and Japanese. Chinese and English, though both of them are SVO languages, have very different properties.

Proceedings of the 1st Workshop on Asian Translation (WAT2014), pages 77–82,
Tokyo, Japan, 4th October 2014.

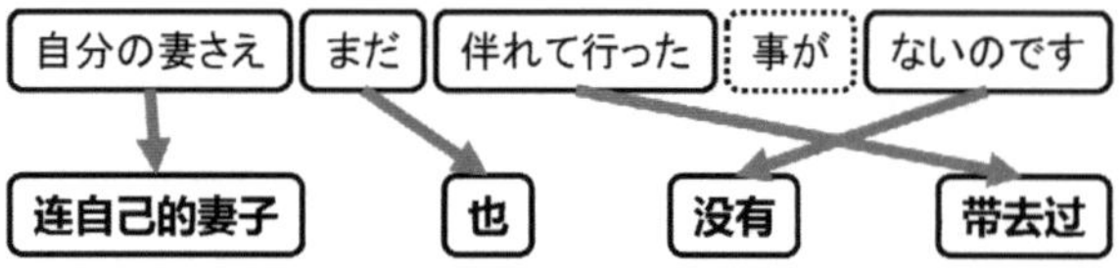

Figure 1: *Japanese tends to use formal noun (in dash-line box) to "wrap" a long clause.*

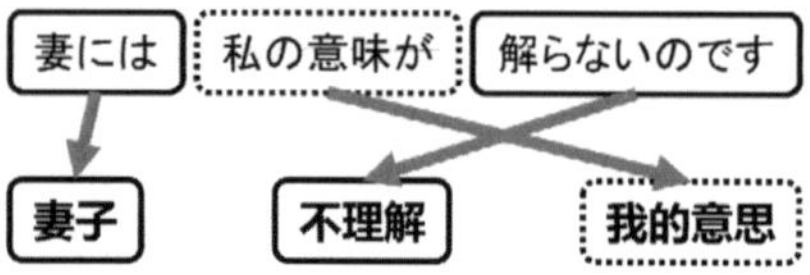

Figure 2: *A nominative phrase in Japanese turns to be an accusative phrase in Chinese.*

2 Character of Chinese and Japanese

In Ding et al. (2014), they proposed three kinds of verb, noun, and copula rules to arrange the order of Japanese chunks[1], with further two rules of morphemes to achieve a more correct pre-reordering. However, their system can not directly applied on Japanese-to-Chinese. Generally, Chinese shares much more similar characters with Japanese than English does, as listed in follows.

- Chinese is head-final in noun phrases, just as Japanese.
- Chinese has no clear boundary between verbs and prepositions. The coverb and serial verb constructions are common in Chinese, which somewhat like Japanese.

Although it seems that the pre-reordering for Japanese-to-Chinese may be easier than the case of Japanese-to-English, there are factors turning the case more complex, as listed in follows.

- Chinese has a strong tendency to avoid long attributes before nouns, while long attributes are acceptable in Japanese, especially for the *formal nouns* in Japanese (Fig. 1).
- Between Chinese and Japanese, the transitive verbs and intransitive verbs are not in accordance in some cases. Essentially, case frame of verbs are not marched well between the two languages (Fig. 2).

According to the mentioned issues, the pre-reordering cannot be conducted by only seeing specific Japanese functional morphemes, such as various case-markers, which are often used in many Japanese-to-English pre-reordering approaches. We design three new inter-chunk rules and modified the intra/extra-rules based on Ding et al. (2014).

[1] i.e. *bunsetsu*

3 Proposed Approach

We use three inter-chunk rules, classified by the corresponding head morpheme in a head chunk. They are *formal-noun rule*, *stative-verb rule* and *dynamic-verb rule*.

Formal-noun rule

Head-initialization is conducted. We only apply the rule to chunks with the formal noun *koto* as its head morpheme.

Stative-verb rule

The modifier chunk with nominative case-marker *ga* is moved after the head chunk. We only apply the rule to chunks with a verb head among *aru*, *iru*, and *dekiru* as its head morpheme.

Dynamic-verb rule

The following modifier chunks are moved after the head chunk.

- with an accusative case-marker *wo*
- with a quotation particle *to*
- with a formal noun as a head morpheme

We apply the rule to chunks with a verb except the three verbs used in the stative-verb rule, as its head morpheme.

We also use extra/intra-chunk rules to arrange certain functional morphemes.

Intra-chunk rule

Auxiliary verbs, except *ta* and copula morphemes, are moved before head morpheme within a chunk.

Extra-chunk rule

Functional morphemes attached to nouns, except genitive case-marker *no* and parallel markers, are moved before the governing range of the chunk.

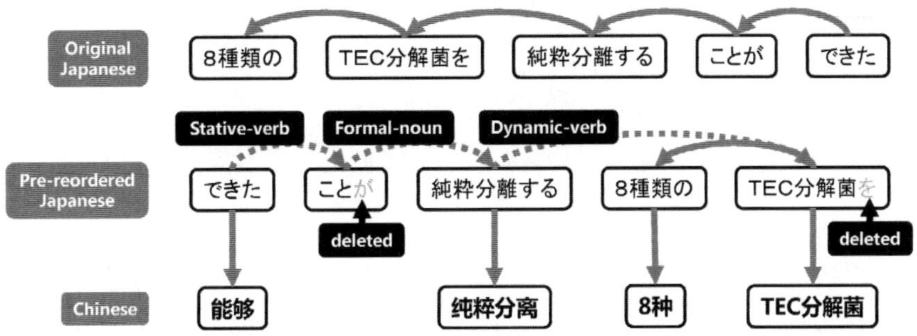

Figure 3: *Example of three inter-chunk rules: formal-noun rule, stative-verb rule and dynamic-verb rule. The alignment between pre-reordered Japanese and Chinese is manually aligned. By the three rules, Morphemes of Japanese are arranged in a Chinese-like order.*

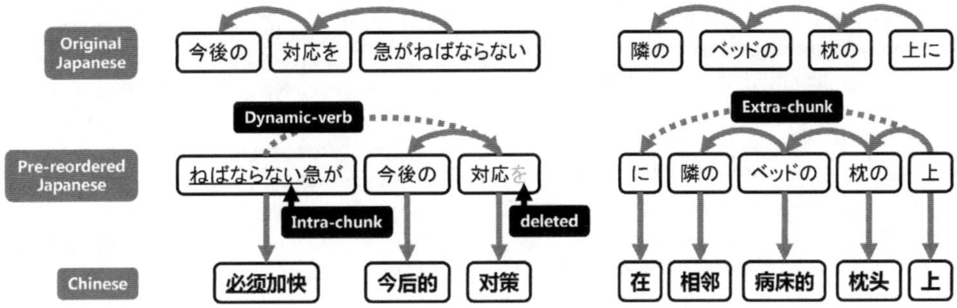

Figure 4: *Examples of Intra- and Extra-chunk rules. The left example shows an intra-chunk move within a verb chunk, leading to a more correct reordering of Japanese functional morphemes, where the underlined parts are corresponding translation. The right example shows an extra-chunk move. A Japanese post-positioned case-marker is arranged to the left-most position of the range it governs. This move makes the Japanese postposition phrase have an identical order to the Chinese preposition phrase.*

We further delete several Japanese functional morphemes which do not have exact Chinese translations. They are as follows.

- topic marker *wa*
- nominative case-marker *ga*
- accusative case-marker *wo*
- conjunctive particle *te*

We illustrate examples of our pre-reordering approach in Figs. 3 and 4.

4 Experiment

We tested our approach on the ASPEC-JC data (Nakazawa et al., 2014). For the source side Japanese sentences, we used MeCab (IPA dictionary)[2] for morpheme analysis, CaboCha[3] (Kudo and Matsumoto, 2002) for chunking and dependency parsing. We used the Stanford Chinese Word Segmenter[4] (Tseng et al., 2005) with the *Chinese Penn Treebank standard* (CTB) to seg-

[2]http://mecab.googlecode.com/svn/trunk/mecab/doc/index.html

[3]https://code.google.com/p/cabocha/

[4]http://www-nlp.stanford.edu/software/segmenter.shtml

ment each Chinese sentence. We used the phrase-based (PB) translation system in Moses[5] (Koehn et al., 2007) as a baseline SMT system. Word alignment was automatically generated by GIZA++[6] (Och and Ney, 2003) with the default setting of Moses, and symmetrized by the *grow-diag-final-and* heuristics (Koehn et al., 2003). In phrase extraction, the *max-phrase-length* was 7 with *GoodTuring* option in scoring. The language model used in decoding is an interpolated modified Kneser-Ney discounted 5-gram model, trained on the English side of the training corpus by SRILM[7] (Stolcke, 2002). In decoding, the *distortion-limit* was 9. The MERT (Och, 2003) was used to tune the feature weights on the development set and the translation performance was evaluated on the test set with the tuned weights. We used identical decoding settings on development and test sets.

Our approach reached a test set BLEU of 28.18 with CTB segmentation in the final evaluation, which had a slight improvement compared with the 28.01 of the organizer's PB SMT baseline. As to the reordering measure RIBES, our approach reached a score of 0.8087, which had a mediocre improvement compared with the organizer's 0.7926. In the human evaluation, our approach also had an improvement of 6.5 percent according to the organizer's evaluation score.

5 Discussion

In a further investigation, we used the Kendall's τ (Isozaki et al., 2012) on training data as an automatic measure, to investigate the difference in word order between Chinese and Japanese and the effect of our pre-reordering approach.

We discovered that the baseline Japanese-to-Chinese word alignment already had an average τ of 0.847 and our approach only improved the score to a slightly higher one of 0.865, which explained why our pre-reordering approach cannot lead to a significant improvement. In Isozaki et al. (2012), their pre-reordering approach (head finalization) improves the average τ from 0.43 to 0.75 in English-to-Japanese translation and In Ding et al. (2014), their pre-reordering approach improves the average τ from 0.49 to 0.67 in Japanese-to-English translation. However, the τ between Chinese and Japanese is very high even without pre-reordering, which suggests Japanese has a much more similar word order with Chinese than English. Then, we conducted more comparisons. We calculated the average τ of French and English, which are usually referred as a language pair with similar word order, on Europarl V7 data[8] (Koehn, 2005). As a result, the score is 0.898, which is not significantly higher than the 0.847 between Chinese and Japanese in our experiment. We further calculated an average τ between Chinese and Japanese on a parallel corpus with 400,000 sentences crawled from Internet[9] and the score decreased to 0.764, which, however, is still relatively high. So we conclude that Chinese and Japanese can be classified as a language pair with *fairly similar* word order but not as a language pair with *significantly different* word order.

As to the phenomenon, we consider a main reason is that Chinese is not a *typical* SVO language. Chinese can even have a SOV word order with the help of a specific particle *ba* preceding the object. As a typical *topic-prominent language*, the word order in Chinese is affected more by semantic constraints than by syntactic ones. We show an example in Fig. 5 to illustrate the strengths and weaknesses of our approach.

From the above discussion, we conclude that Japanese-to-Chinese is a relatively easier translation task than Japanese-to-English, and thus a state-of-the-art PB SMT system can achieve an acceptable performance. On the other hand, rather than the word order problem, which we have found not such a serious issue, we consider the errors in word alignment around Japanese functional morphemes is a critical issue in our experiment. Japanese has a sophisticated system of case-markers, particles, and auxiliary verbs, which are deeply tangled with its syntax and semantics. However, these functional morphemes usually have not exactly corresponding translations in Chinese, and an unsupervised automatic word aligner tends to scatter the alignment of them. We assume that using more explicit syntax information in training and decoding phrases of an SMT system may improve the alignment of these functional morphemes and lead to a better performance in translation quality.

[5] `http://www.statmt.org/moses/`

[6] `http://code.google.com/p/giza-pp/`

[7] `http://www.speech.sri.com/projects/srilm/`

[8] `http://www.statmt.org/europarl/`

[9] `http://japanese.donga.com/`

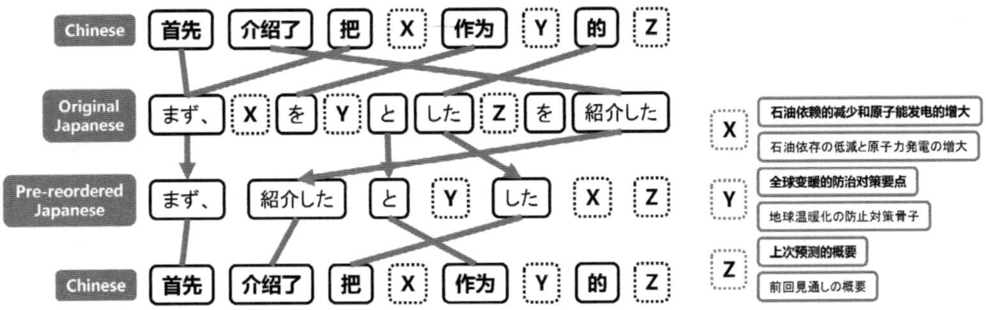

Figure 5: *Example of pre-reordering for a Japanese sentence and the automatically generated word alignment of its Chinese translation. The upper row and the lower row are identical Chinese sentence. The two rows in middle are original and pre-reordered Japanese sentences. X, Y, Z are monotonic noun phrases not affecting the sentence structures. The pre-reordering approach can move the final-positioned verb properly and lead to a more correct alignment of functional words. However, the original Japanese sentence has already had a similar word order as the Chinese sentence except the final verb, while the pre-reordering conducted a rigid reordering of swapping X and Y, which leads to an excess move.*

6 Conclusion and Future Work

We propose a rule-based pre-reordering approach for Japanese-to-Chinese SMT, using the dependency parsing of source-side Japanese sentences. The approach can bring a mediocre improvement in automatic and human evaluation metrics. We investigate the experimental results and discover that Chinese and Japanese actually have relatively similar word orders. It seems that the proposed approach is too rigid to handle the word reordering of Japanese-to-Chinese translation task. We plan to conduct deeper investigation of the two languages and design more flexible pre-reordering rules.

Acknowledgment

We thank Mitsuo Yoshida for providing parallel data on Japanese and Chinese crawled form Internet, which helps us to investigate the characters of the two languages.

References

Han Dan, Katsuhito Sudoh, Xianchao Wu, Kevin Duh, Hajime Tsukada, and Masaaki Nagata. 2012. Head finalization reordering for Chinese-to-Japanese machine translation. In *Proc. of SSST*, pages 57–66.

Chenchen Ding, Keisuke Sakanushi, Hirona Touji, and Mikio Yamamoto. 2014. Dependency tree-based pre-reordering rules for statistical Japanese-to-English machine translation. In *Proc. of ANLP*, pages 963–966. (In Japanese).

Sho Hoshino, Yusuke Miyao, Katsuhito Sudoh, and Masaaki Nagata. 2013. Two-stage pre-ordering for Japanese-to-English statistical machine translation. In *Proc. of IJCNLP*, pages 1062–1066.

Hideki Isozaki, Katsuhito Sudoh, Hajime Tsukada, and Kevin Duh. 2012. HPSG-based preprocessing for English-to-Japanese translation. *ACM Transactions on Asian Language Information Processing*, 11(3). Article 8.

Jason Katz-Brown and Michael Collins. 2008. Syntactic reordering in preprocessing for Japanese English translation: MIT system description for NTCIR-7 patent translation task. In *Proc. of NTCIR*, pages 409–414.

Philipp Koehn, Franz Josef Och, and Daniel Marcu. 2003. Statistical phrase-based translation. In *Proc. of HTL-NAACL*, pages 48–54.

Philipp Koehn, Hieu Hoang, Alexandra Birch, Chris Callison-Burch, Marcello Federico, Nicola Bertoldi, Brooke Cowan, Wade Shen, Christine Moran, Richard Zens, Chris Dyer, Ondrej Bojar, Alexandra Constantin, and Evan Herbst. 2007. Moses: Open source toolkit for statistical machine translation. In *Proc. of ACL*, pages 177–180.

Philipp Koehn. 2005. Europarl: A parallel corpus for statistical machine translation. In *Proc. of MT summit*, pages 79–86.

Mamoru Komachi, Yuji Matsumoto, and Masaaki Nagata. 2006. Phrase reordering for statistical machine translation based on predicate-argument structure. In *Proc. of IWSLT*, pages 77–82.

Taku Kudo and Yuji Matsumoto. 2002. Japanese dependency analysis using cascaded chunking. In *Proc. of CoNLL*, pages 63–69.

Toshiaki Nakazawa, Hideya Mino, Isao Goto, Sadao Kurohashi, and Eiichiro Sumita. 2014. Overview of the 1st Workshop on Asian Translation. In *Proc. of WAT*.

Franz Josef Och and Hermann Ney. 2003. A systematic comparison of various statistical alignment models. *Computational Linguistics*, 29(1):19–51.

Franz Josef Och. 2003. Minimum error rate training in statistical machine translation. In *Proc. of ACL*, pages 160–167.

Andreas Stolcke. 2002. SRILM–an extensible language modeling toolkit. In *Proc. of ICSLP 2002*, pages 901–904.

Katsuhito Sudoh, Kevin Duh, Hajime Tsukada, Masaaki Nagata, Xianchao Wu, Takuya Matsuzaki, and Jun'ichi Tsujii. 2011. NTT-UT statistical machine translation in NTCIR-9 PatentMT. In *Proc. of NTCIR*, pages 585–592.

Huihsin Tseng, Pichuan Chang, Galen Andrew, Daniel Jurafsky, and Christopher Manning. 2005. A conditional random field word segmenter. In *SIGHAN 2005, Workshop on Chinese Language Processing*, volume 171.

KyotoEBMT System Description for the 1st Workshop on Asian Translation

John Richardson[†] Fabien Cromières[‡] Toshiaki Nakazawa[‡] Sadao Kurohashi[†]
[†]Graduate School of Informatics, Kyoto University, Kyoto 606-8501
[‡]Japan Science and Technology Agency, Kawaguchi-shi, Saitama 332-0012
john@nlp.ist.i.kyoto-u.ac.jp, {fabien, nakazawa}@pa.jst.jp,
kuro@i.kyoto-u.ac.jp

Abstract

This paper introduces the KyotoEBMT Example-Based Machine Translation framework. Our system uses a *tree-to-tree* approach, employing syntactic dependency analysis for both source and target languages in an attempt to preserve non-local structure. The effectiveness of our system is maximized with online example matching and a flexible decoder. Evaluation demonstrates BLEU scores competitive with state-of-the-art SMT baselines. The system implementation is available as open-source.

1 Introduction

Corpus-based approaches have become a major focus of Machine Translation research. We present here a fully-fledged Example-Based Machine Translation (EBMT) platform making use of both source-language and target-language dependency structure. This paradigm has been explored comparatively less, as studies on Syntactic-based SMT/EBMT tend to focus on constituent trees rather than dependency trees, and on tree-to-string rather than tree-to-tree approaches. Furthermore, we employ separate dependency parsers for each language rather than projecting the dependencies from one language to another, as in (Quirk et. al, 2005).

The dependency structure information is used end-to-end: for improving the quality of the alignment of the translation examples, for constraining the translation rule extraction and for guiding the decoding. We believe that dependency structure, which considers more than just local context, is important in order to generate fluent and accurate translations of complex sentences across distant language pairs.

Our experiments focus on technical domain translation for Japanese-Chinese and Japanese-English, however our implementation is applicable to any domain and language pair for which there exist translation examples and dependency parsers.

A further unique characteristic of our system is that, again contrary to the majority of similar systems, it does not rely on precomputation of translation rules. Instead it matches each input sentence to the full database of translation examples before extracting translation rules online. This has the merit of maximizing the information available when creating and combining translation rules, while retaining the ability to produce excellent translations for input sentences similar to an existing translation example.

The system is mostly developed in C++ and incorporates a web-based translation interface for ease of use. The web interface (see Figure 1) also displays information useful for error analysis such as the list of translation examples used. Experiments are facilitated through the inclusion of a curses-based graphical interface for performing tuning and evaluation. The decoder supports multiple threads.

The system has been made available as open-source. The code can be downloaded from http://nlp.ist.i.kyoto-u.ac.jp/kyotoebmt/.

2 System Overview

Figure 2 shows the basic structure of the Kyoto EBMT translation pipeline.

The training process begins with parsing and aligning parallel sentences from the training corpus. Alignment uses a Bayesian subtree alignment model based on dependency

Proceedings of the 1st Workshop on Asian Translation (WAT2014), pages 83–88,
Tokyo, Japan, 4th October 2014.

Figure 1: A screenshot of the web interface showing a Japanese-English translation. The interface provides the source and target side dependency tree, as well as the list of examples used with their alignments. The web interface facilitates easy and intuitive error analysis, and can be used as a tool for computer-aided translation.

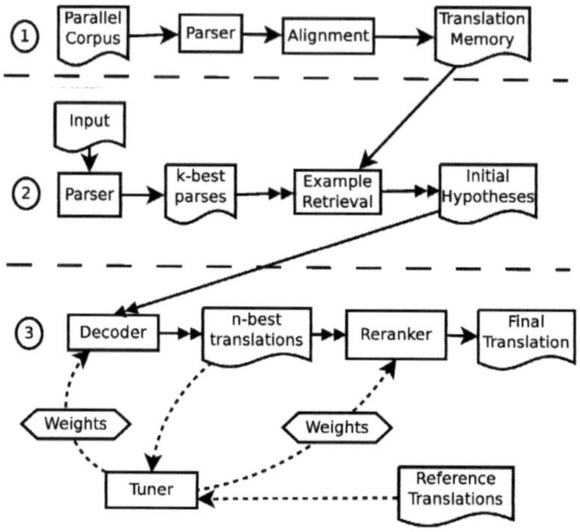

Figure 2: The translation pipeline can be roughly divided in 3 steps. Step 1 is the creation of the example database, trained from a parallel corpus. Step 2 is the k-best parsing of an input sentence and the generation of k sets of initial hypotheses. Step 3 consists in decoding and reranking. The tuning of the weights for decoding and reranking is done by a modified version of step 3. The double arrows indicate the parallel processing of each of the k parse of the input sentence.

trees. This contains a tree-based reordering model and can capture non-local reorderings, which sequential word-based models often cannot handle effectively. The alignments are then used to build an example database ('translation memory') containing 'examples' or 'treelets' that form the hypotheses to be combined during decoding.

Translation is performed by first parsing an input sentence then searching for treelets matching entries in the example database. The retrieved treelets are combined by a decoder that optimizes a log linear model score. Finally, a reranker select an optimal translation in the n-best list provided by the decoder using additional non-local features (see section 6).

In order to be more robust with respect to parse errors, the input sentence can be parsed into a k-best list of posible parses. Each parse is then translated separately and all translations are merged before the final reranking step (see section 7).

The example retrieval and decoding steps are explained in more detail in sections 3 and 4 respectively. The choice of features and the tuning of the log linear model is described in section 5.

Figure 3 shows the process of combining examples matching the input tree to create an output sentence.

3 Example retrieval and translation hypothesis construction

An important characteristic of our system is that we do not extract and store translation rules in advance: the alignment of translation examples is performed offline. However, for a given input sentence i, the steps for finding examples partially matching i and extracting their translation hypotheses is an online process. This approach could be considered to be more faithful to the original EBMT approach advocated by Nagao (1984). It has already been proposed for phrase-based (Callison-Burch et al., 2005), hierarchical (Lopez, 2007), and syntax-based (Cromières and Kurohashi, 2011) systems. It does not however, seem to be very commonly integrated in syntax-based MT.

This approach has several benefits. The first

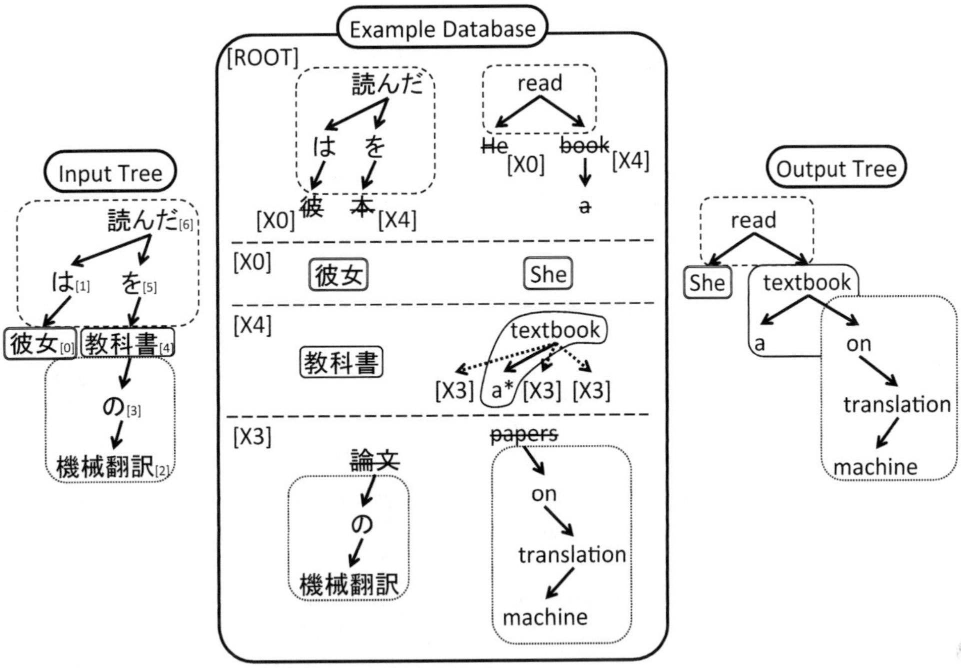

Figure 3: The process of translation. The source sentence is parsed and matching subtrees from the example database are retrieved. From the examples, we extract translation hypotheses than can contain optional target words and several position for each non-terminals. For example the translation hypothesis containing "textbook" has three possible position for the non-terminal X3 (as a left-child before "a", as a left-child after "a" or as a right-child). The translation hypotheses are then combined during decoding. Choice of optional words and final Non-Terminal positions is also done during decoding.

is that we are not required to impose a limit on the size of translation hypotheses. Systems extracting rules in advance typically restrict the size and number of extracted rules for fear of becoming unmanageable. In particular, if an input sentence is the same or very similar to one of our translation examples, we will be able to retrieve a perfect translation. A second advantage is that we can make use of the full context of the example to assign features and scores to each translation hypothesis.

The main drawback of our approach is that it can be computationally more expensive to retrieve arbitrarily large matchings in the example database online than it is to match precomputed rules. We use the techniques described in (Cromières and Kurohashi, 2011) to perform this step as efficiently as possible.

Once we have found an example translation (s, t) for which s partially matches i, we proceed to extract a translation hypothesis from it. A translation hypothesis is defined as a generic translation rule for a part p of the input sentence that is represented as a target-language treelet, with non-terminals representing the insertion positions for the translations of other parts of the sentence. A translation hypothesis is created from a translation example as follows:

1. We project the part of s that is matched into the target side t using the alignment of s and t. This is trivial if each word of s and t is aligned, but this is not typically the case. Therefore our translation hypotheses will often have some target words/nodes marked as *optionals*: this means that we will decide if they should be added to the final translation only at the moment of combination.

2. We insert the non-terminals as child nodes of the projected subtree. This is

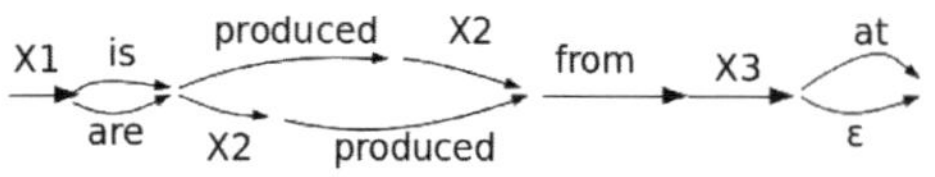

Figure 4: A translation hypothesis endoded as a lattice. This representation allows us to handle efficiently the ambiguities of our translation rules. Note that each path in this lattice corresponds to different choices of insertion position for X2, morphological forms of "be", and the optional insertion of "at".

simple if i, s and t have the same structure and are perfectly aligned, but again this is not typically the case. A consequence is that we will sometimes have *several possible insertion positions* for each non-terminal. The choice of insertion position is again made during combination.

4 Decoding

After having extracted translation hypotheses for as many parts of the input tree as possible, we need to decide how to select and combine them. Our approach here is similar to what has been proposed for Corpus-Based Machine Translation. We first choose a number of features and create a linear model scoring each possible combination of hypotheses (see Section 5). We then attempt to find the combination that maximizes this model score.

The combination of rules is constrained by the structure of the input dependency tree. If we only consider local features[1], then a simple bottom-up dynamic programming approach can efficiently find the optimal combination with linear $O(|\mathcal{H}|)$ complexity[2]. However, non-local features (such as language models) will force us to prune the search space. This pruning is done efficiently through a variation of cube-pruning (Chiang, 2007). We use KenLM[3] (Heafield, 2011) for computing the target language model score. Decoding is made more efficient by using some of the more advanced features of KenLM such as state-reduction ((Li and Khudanpur, 2008), (Heafield et al., 2011)) and rest-cost estimations(Heafield et al., 2012).

[1]The score of a combination will be the sum of the local scores of each translation hypothesis.

[2]$\mathcal{H}$ = set of translation hypotheses

[3]http://kheafield.com/code/kenlm/

Compared with the original cube-pruning algorithm, our decoder is designed to handle an arbitrary number of non-terminals. In addition, as we have seen in Section 3, the translation hypotheses we initially extract from examples are ambiguous in term of which target word is going to be used and which will be the final position of each non-terminal. In order to handle such ambiguities, we use a lattice-based internal representation that can encode them efficiently (see Figure 4). This lattice representation also allows the decoder to make choices between various morphological variations of a word (e.g. be/is/are). We use the decoding algorithm described in (Cromieres and Kurohashi, 2014).

5 Features and Tuning

During decoding we use a linear model to score each possible combination of hypotheses. This linear model is based on a linear combination of both local features (local to each translation hypothesis) and non-local features (such as a 5-gram language model score of the final translation). The decoder considers in total a combination of 42 features, a selection of which are given below.

- Example penalty and example size
- Translation probability
- Language model score
- Optional words added/removed

The optimal weights for each feature are estimated using the implementation of k-best batch MIRA (Cherry and Foster, 2012) included in Moses.

6 Reranking

We reranked the n-best output of our system using an additional two language models: a standard 7-gram language model with Modified Kneser-Ney smoothing and a Recurrent Neural Network Language Model (RNNLM) (Mikolov et. al, 2010). The RNNLM model was trained with hidden layer size 200, and 5000 sentences from the training fold were used as validation data.

Reranking was conducted by first calculating the various language model scores for each translation in the n-best list. These features were added to those used in the first round of tuning, then one final iteration of tuning was run. The tuning algorithm and settings were the same as for standard tuning. This retuning step was added in order to find an optimal combination of the two additional LMs with related features such as sentence length and the score given by the 5-gram language model used inside the decoder.

7 K-best parsing

We found that the quality of the source-side dependency parsing had an important impact on translation quality. Unfortunately, parsing errors are unavoidable. Chinese parsing is maybe especially challenging and our Chinese parser still produces a significant number of parsing errors. In order to mitigate this problem, we use a k-best list of parses of the input sentence. Each parse is translated in parallel, and the list of translation thus obtained is merged before the reranking step. In the future, we intend to move from a k-best list representation of multiple parses to a more compact and efficient forest representation. Furthermore, we will also have to consider multiple parses for all the translation examples (and not just the input sentence).

8 Experiments

The following dependency parsers were used. The scores in parentheses are the approximate parsing accuracies (micro-average), which were evaluated by hand on a random subset of sentences from the test data. The parsers were trained on domains different to those used in the experiments.

- English: NLParser[4] (92%) (Charniak and Johnson, 2005)
- Japanese: KNP (96%) (Kawahara and Kurohashi, 2006)
- Chinese: SKP (88%) (Shen et al., 2012)

K-best dependency parsing was done with k set to 20.

[4]Converted to dependency parses with in-house tool.

8.1 Results

The results shown are for evaluation on the test set after tuning. Tuning was conducted over 20 iterations on the development set using an n-best list of length 500.

9 Conclusion

We have described the Kyoto example-based translation system. It uses both source and target dependency analysis, as well as online example retrieving, allowing the availability of full translation examples at translation time.

We believe that the use of dependency parsing is important for accurate translation across distant language pairs, especially in settings such as ours with many long sentences. We have designed a complete translation framework around this idea, using dependency-parsed trees at each step from alignment to example retrieval to example combination.

References

Eugene Charniak and Mark Johnson. 2005. Coarse-to-Fine n-Best Parsing and MaxEnt Discriminative Reranking. In *Proceedings of the 43rd Annual Meeting of the Association for Computational Linguistics, ACL 2005.*

Fabien Cromières and Sadao Kurohashi. 2011. Efficient retrieval of tree translation examples for syntax-based machine translation. In *Proceedings of the 2011 Conference on Empirical Methods in Natural Language Processing.*

Isao Goto, Ka Po Chow, Bin Lu, Eiichiro Sumita and Benjamin Tsou. 2013. Overview of the Patent Machine Translation Task at the NTCIR-10 Workshop. In *Proceedings of the 10th NTCIR Workshop Meeting on Evaluation of Information Access Technologies (NTCIR-10).*

Daisuke Kawahara and Sadao Kurohashi. 2006. A Fully-Lexicalized Probabilistic Model for Japanese Syntactic and Case Structure Analysis. In *Proceedings of the Human Language Technology Conference of the NAACL.*

Makoto Nagao. 1984. A framework of a mechanical translation between Japanese and English by analogy principle. In *A. Elithorn and R. Banerji. Artificial and Human Intelligence.*

Toshiaki Nakazawa and Sadao Kurohashi. 2012. Alignment by bilingual generation and monolingual derivation. In *Proceedings of COLING 2012.*

Language Pair	Reranking	BLEU	RIBES	HUMAN
JA–EN	No	20.60	70.12	21.50
	Yes	21.07	69.90	25.00
EN–JA	No	29.76	75.21	33.75
	Yes	31.09	75.96	38.00
JA–ZH	No	27.21	79.13	-0.75
	Yes	27.67	78.83	-8.75
ZH–JA	No	33.57	80.10	6.00
	Yes	34.75	80.26	7.50

Table 1: Scores

Mo Shen, Daisuke Kawahara and Sadao Kurohashi. 2012. A Reranking Approach for Dependency Parsing with Variable-sized Subtree Features. In *Proceedings of 26th Pacific Asia Conference on Language Information and Computing.*

Chris Callison-Burch, Colin Bannard, and Josh Schroeder. 2005. Scaling phrase-based statistical machine translation to larger corpora and longer phrases. In *Proceedings of the 43rd Annual Meeting on Association for Computational Linguistics*, pages 255–262. Association for Computational Linguistics, 2005.

Colin Cherry and George Foster. 2012. Batch Tuning Strategies for Statistical Machine Translation. In *HLT-NAACL*, 2012.

David Chiang. 2007. Hierarchical phrase-based translation. In *Computational Linguistics.*

Cromieres Fabien and Sadao Kurohashi. 2014. Translation Rules with Right-Hand Side Lattices. In *Proceedings of EMNLP 2014*

Kenneth Heafield. 2011. KenLM: faster and smaller language model queries. In *Proceedings of the EMNLP 2011 Sixth Workshop on Statistical Machine Translation*, 2011.

Kenneth Heafield, Hieu Hoang, Philipp Koehn, Tetsuo Kiso, and Marcello Federico. 2011. Left language model state for syntactic machine translation. In *Proceedings of the International Workshop on Spoken Language Translation*, 2011.

Kenneth Heafield, Philipp Koehn, and Alon Lavie. 2012. Language model rest costs and space-efficient storage. In *Proceedings of the Joint Conference on Empirical Methods in Natural Language Processing and Computational Natural Language Learning*, 2012.

Zhifei Li and Sanjeev Khudanpur. 2008. A scalable decoder for parsing-based machine translation with equivalent language model state maintenance. In *Proceedings of the Second Workshop on Syntax and Structure in Statistical Translation.* Association for Computational Linguistics, 2008.

Adam Lopez. 2007. Hierarchical phrase-based translation with suffix arrays. In *EMNLP-CoNLL*, 2007.

Tomas Mikolov, Martin Karafiat, Lukas Burget, Jan Cernocky and Sanjeev Khudanpur. 2010. Recurrent Neural Network Based Language Model. In *Proceedings of the 11th Annual Conference of the International Speech Communication Association*, 2010.

Chris Quirk, Arul Menezes, and Colin Cherry. 2005. Dependency Treelet Translation: Syntactically Informed Phrasal SMT. In *Proceedings of the 43rd Annual Meeting on Association for Computational Linguistics.* Association for Computational Linguistics, 2005.